# SHAKESPEARE'S

COMEDY OF

# THE TEMPEST.

EDITED, WITH NOTES,

BY

WILLIAM J. ROLFE, A.M.,

FORMERLY HEAD MASTER OF THE HIGH SCHOOL, CAMBRIDGE, MASS.

*WITH ENGRAVINGS.*

*NEW YORK*:

HARPER & BROTHERS, PUBLISHERS,

FRANKLIN SQUARE.

1881.

Entered according to Act of Congress, in the year 1871, by

HARPER & BROTHERS,

In the Office of the Librarian of Congress, at Washington.

# PREFACE.

THE plan of this edition has been already explained in the Preface to *The Merchant of Venice.* The notes on this play also were written several years ago, but have been carefully revised before being sent to the press.

The "expurgation" of the text consists in the removal of only three or four lines. I might, perhaps, have decided to strike out a few other passages, had they not been so interwoven with the *thought* of the play that too much of the context would have to be sacrificed with them.

The enlarged edition of Abbott's "Shakespearian Grammar" was published just as *The Merchant of Venice* was going to press, and I was able to make but limited use of it in the final revision of my notes. It seems to me the best work on the English of Shakespeare that has yet appeared, and in these notes on *The Tempest* I have referred to it frequently. One of its chief merits is the very full citation of illustrative passages. Shakespeare is thus made his own commentator, and he often proves a far better one than any of his editors or critics.

The "Philadelphia edition," to which I have often referred, is the "Notes of Studies on *The Tempest,* from the Minutes of the Shakespeare Society of Philadelphia for 1864–65," of which sixty copies were privately printed for the society in 1866. It is much to be regretted that these valuable Notes are accessible to only a favored few among the students of Shakespeare, but we may hope that Mr. Furness, the Secretary of the Society, will ere long make them more widely known by incorporating them into his "New Variorum Edition" of this play.

References to the notes have not been inserted *in the text* of either *The Merchant of Venice* or the present play, partly because they would have been so numerous as to disfigure the page, and partly because they seem to me of no special use. For the school-room they are worse than useless. While preparing his lesson, the pupil is not likely to overlook any thing in the notes that will help him; and at the recitation, neither the notes themselves, nor any thing that may serve as a guide-board to them, should be directly before his eyes.

With regard to this and all other features of this edition, I have been guided by my experience as a teacher, while I have aimed at the same time to keep constantly in view the wants and the tastes of the general reader. The favor with which *The Merchant of Venice* has been received, both by teachers and by the public, encourages me in bringing out this second number of the series, which I trust may prove in some respects even more worthy of their approval.

*Cambridge*, June 1, 1871.

# CONTENTS.

"Thy groans
Did make wolves howl."

"BERMOOTHES."

# INTRODUCTION

TO

# THE TEMPEST.

## I. HISTORY OF THE PLAY.

*The Tempest* occupies the first nineteen pages of the Folio of 1623, and no earlier edition of the play has been discovered. It is not unlikely, as White has suggested, that "it was made the leading play, as being one of the latest and most admired works of its author." Mr. Joseph Hunter* has attempted to show that it was written as early as 1596; but the commentators generally agree that the date cannot be put earlier than 1603, and that it was probably as late as 1611.

* *New Illustrations of Shakespeare* (1845), vol. i. pp. 122–157.

The speech of Gonzalo (ii. 1), "I' th' commonwealth I would by contraries," etc.,* is manifestly copied from a passage in Florio's translation of Montaigne, which appeared in 1603. We must therefore believe that the play was written after that time, unless we adopt the hypothesis that Shakespeare had seen Florio's work in manuscript. The *Accounts of the Revels at Court* state that *The Tempest* was performed before King James, Nov. 1st, 1611; but the entry, which is as follows, is now known to be a forgery:

| By the Kings players. | Hallomas nyght was presented att Whithall before y^e^ Kinges Ma^tie^ a play called the Tempest. |
|---|---|

"To this positive external testimony,"† says White, "are to be added some external probabilities. First, in the occurrence of a passage in the Introduction to Ben Jonson's *Bartholomew Fair*, written between 1612 and 1614, which has a hit, not necessarily ill-humored, at those who have 'a *Servant-monster*' in their *dramatis personæ*, and 'beget *Tales, Tempests*, and such like *Drolleries*,' where the allusion to *The Tempest* is too plain to be mistaken—an allusion which would be made only when the impression of that play was fresh in the public mind. Next, in the publication by Sil[vester] Jourdan of a quarto pamphlet entitled 'A Discovery of the Barmvdas, otherwise called the Ile of Divels: by Sir Thomas Gates, Sir George Sommers, and Captayne Newport, with diuers others. London, 1610.' This pamphlet tells of the tempest which scattered the fleet commanded by Somers and Gates, and the happy discovery, by some of the shipwrecked, of land which proved to be the Bermudas. It alludes to the general belief that these islands 'were *never* inhabited by any Christian or Heathen people,' being 'reputed a most *prodigious and enchanted* place,' adding that, nevertheless, those who were cast away upon them, and lived there nine months, found the air temperate and the country 'abundantly fruitful of all fit nec-

* See note, p. 124. † This was written before the forgery was detected.

essaries for the sustentation and preservation of man's life.' *Prospero's* command to *Ariel* 'to fetch dew from the still-vex'd Bermoothes' makes it certain that the Bermudas are not the scene of *The Tempest*, though, strangely enough, it has produced the contrary impression on many minds; but this reference to these islands, and allusion to their storm-vexed coast, connects itself naturally with the publication of Jourdan's narrative. It is highly probable, therefore, that *The Tempest* was written about 1611.

"The thoughtful reader will, however, find in the compact simplicity of its structure, and in the chastened grandeur of its diction and the lofty severity of its tone of thought, tempered although the one is with Shakespeare's own enchanting sweetness, and the other with that most human tenderness which is the peculiar trait of his mind, sufficient evidence that this play is the fruit of his genius in its full maturity."

## II. THE SOURCES OF THE PLOT.

Shakespeare usually founded his plays upon some well-known history or romance, and the plot of *The Tempest*, though the critics have not succeeded in tracing it to its source, was doubtless borrowed from some old Italian or Spanish novel. Collins, the poet, told Thomas Warton that he had seen such a novel, with the title of *Aurelio and Isabella*, and that it was "printed in Italian, Spanish, French, and English, in 1588;" and Boswell says that a friend of his assured him that, some years before, he had "actually perused an Italian novel which answered to Collins's description." But Collins was insane when he made the statement, and Boswell's friend may have been mistaken; at any rate, the romance has not yet been found. There is an early German play (published in 1618) called *Die Schöne Sidea*, by Jacob Ayrer, a notary of Nuremberg, the plot of which is somewhat like that of *The Tempest*, and this has led several critics to suppose that the two were drawn from the same source; but the resemblance is hardly close enough to justify the conclusion. If there is any connection between the plays, it is possible that Ayrer had seen *The Tempest*, or a translation of it. Although, according to Eschenburg, no reference to Shakespeare has been found in German literature farther back than 1682, it is certain that English plays were translated into German as early as 1600.

"As to the actual scene of *The Tempest*, that is in the realms of fancy. Mr. Hunter has contended that Lampedusa, 'an island in the Mediterranean, lying not far out of a ship's course passing from Tunis to Naples,' and which is uninhabited, and supposed by sailors to be enchanted, was *Prospero's* place of exile. It may have been; though if it were, we would a little rather not believe so. When the great magician at whose beck it rose from the waters broke his staff, the island sunk, and carried *Caliban* down with it."*

## III. CRITICAL COMMENTS ON THE PLAY.

[*From Coleridge's Notes on Shakespeare.*†]

*The Tempest* is a specimen of the purely romantic drama, in which the interest is not historical, or dependent upon fidelity of portraiture, or the natural connection of events; but is a birth of the imagination, and rests only on the coaptation and union of the elements granted to, or assumed by, the poet. It is a species of drama which owes no allegiance to time or space, and in which, therefore, errors of chronology and geography—no mortal sins in any species—are venial faults, and count for nothing. It addresses itself entirely to the imaginative faculty; and although the illusion may be assisted by the effect on the senses of the complicated scenery and decorations of modern times, yet this sort of assistance is dangerous. For the principal and only genuine excitement ought to come from within—from the moved and sympathetic imagination; whereas, where so much is address-

* White. † Coleridge's Works (Harper's ed.), vol. iv. pp. 74 foll.

ed to the mere external senses of seeing and hearing, the spiritual vision is apt to languish, and the attraction from without will withdraw the mind from the proper and only legitimate interest which is intended to spring from within.

The romance opens with a busy scene admirably appropriate to the kind of drama, and giving, as it were, the key-note to the whole harmony. It prepares and initiates the excitement required for the entire piece, and yet does not demand any thing from the spectators which their previous habits had not fitted them to understand. It is the bustle of a tempest, from which the real horrors are abstracted; therefore it is poetical, though not in strictness natural, and is purposely restrained from concentring the interest on itself, but used merely as an induction or tuning for what is to follow.

In the second scene, Prospero's speeches, till the entrance of Ariel, contain the finest example I remember of retrospective narration for the purpose of exciting immediate interest, and putting the audience in possession of all the information necessary for the understanding of the plot. Observe, too, the perfect probability of the moment chosen by Prospero (the very Shakespeare himself, as it were, of the tempest) to open out the truth to his daughter, his own romantic bearing, and how completely any thing that might have been disagreeable to us in the magician is reconcilable and shaded in the humanity and natural feelings of the father. In the very first speech of Miranda the simplicity and tenderness of her character are at once laid open—it would have been lost in direct contact with the agitation of the first scene. . . . .

Ariel has in everything the airy tint which gives the name. And it is worthy of remark that Miranda is never directly brought into comparison with Ariel, lest the natural and human of the one and the supernatural of the other should tend to neutralize each other. Caliban, on the other hand, is all earth, all condensed and gross in feelings and images; he has the dawnings of understanding, without reason or the moral sense; and in him, as in some brute animals, this advance to the intellectual faculties, without the moral sense, is marked by the appearance of vice. For it is in the primacy of the moral being only that man is truly human; in his intellectual powers he is certainly approached by the brutes, and, man's whole system duly considered, those powers cannot be considered other than means to an end, that is, to morality. . . . .

In this play are admirably sketched the vices generally accompanying a low degree of civilization; and in the first scene of the second act Shakespeare has, as in many other places, shown the tendency in bad men to indulge in scorn and contemptuous expressions, as a mode of getting rid of their own uneasy feelings of inferiority to the good, and also, by making the good ridiculous, of rendering the transition of others to wickedness easy. Shakespeare never puts habitual scorn into the mouths of other than bad men, as here in the instance of Antonio and Sebastian. The scene of the intended assassination of Alonso and Gonzalo is an exact counterpart of the scene between Macbeth and his lady, only pitched in a lower key throughout, as designed to be frustrated or concealed, and exhibiting the same profound management in the manner of familiarizing a mind not immediately recipient to the suggestion of guilt, by associating the proposed crime with something ludicrous or out of place—something not habitually matter of reverence. By this kind of sophistry the imagination and fancy are first bribed to contemplate the suggested act, and at length to become acquainted with it. Observe how the effect of this scene is heightened by contrast of another counterpart of it in low life—that between the conspirators, Stephano, Caliban, and Trinculo, in the second scene of the third act, in which there are the same essential characteristics.

In this play, and in this scene of it, are also shown the springs of the vulgar in politics—of that kind of politics which is inwoven with human nature. In his treatment of this subject, wherever it occurs, Shakespeare is quite peculiar. In other writers we find the particular opinions of the individual; . . . but Shakespeare never promulgates any party tenets. He is always the philosopher and the moralist, but, at the same time, with a profound veneration for all the established institutions of society, and for those classes which form the permanent elements of the state—especially never introducing a professional character, as such, otherwise than as respectable. If he must have any name, he should be styled a philosophical aristocrat, delighting in those hereditary institutions which have a tendency to bind one age to another, and in that distinction of ranks of which, although few may be in possession, all enjoy the advantages. Hence, again, you will observe the good nature with which he seems always to make sport with the passions and follies of a mob, as with an irrational animal. He is never angry with it, but hugely content with holding up its absurdities to its face; and sometimes you may trace a tone of almost affectionate superiority, something like that in which a father speaks of the rogueries of a child. See the good-humoured way in which he describes Stephano, passing from the most licentious freedom to absolute despotism over Trinculo and Caliban. The truth is, Shakespeare's characters are all *genera* intensely individualized; the results of meditation, of which observation supplied the drapery and the colours necessary to combine them with each other. He had virtually surveyed all the great component powers and impulses of human nature—had seen that their different combinations and subordinations were in fact the individualizers of men, and showed how their harmony was produced by reciprocal disproportions of excess or deficiency. The language in which these truths are expressed was not drawn from any set fashion, but from the profoundest depths of his moral being, and is therefore for all ages.

[*From Schlegel's "Lectures on Dramatic Literature.*"*]

*The Midsummer Night's Dream* and *The Tempest* may be so far compared together that in both the influence of a wonderful world of spirits is interwoven with the turmoil of human passions and with the farcical adventures of folly. *The Midsummer Night's Dream* is certainly an earlier production; but *The Tempest*, according to all appearance, was written in Shakespeare's later days: hence most critics, on the supposition that the poet must have continued to improve with increasing maturity of mind, have honoured the last piece with a marked preference. I cannot, however, altogether concur with them: the intrinsic merits of these two works are, in my opinion, pretty nearly balanced, and a predilection for the one or the other can only be governed by personal taste. In profound and original characterization the superiority of *The Tempest* is obvious: as a whole, we must always admire the masterly skill which the poet has here displayed in the economy of his means, and the dexterity with which he has disguised his preparations—the scaffoldings for the wonderful aërial structure. . . . .

*The Tempest* has little action or progressive movement; the union of Ferdinand and Miranda is settled at their first interview, and Prospero merely throws apparent obstacles in their way; the shipwrecked band go leisurely about the island; the attempts of Sebastian and Antonio on the life of the King of Naples, and the plot of Caliban and the drunken sailors against Prospero, are nothing but a feint, for we foresee that they will be completely frustrated by the magical skill of the latter; nothing remains, therefore, but the punishment of the guilty by dreadful sights which harrow up their consciences, and then the discovery and final reconciliation. Yet this want of movement is so admirably concealed by the most varied display of the fascinations of poetry and the ex-

* *Bohn's* translation.

hilaration of mirth, the details of the execution are so very attractive, that it requires no small degree of attention to perceive that the *dénouement* is, in some degree, anticipated in the exposition. The history of the loves of Ferdinand and Miranda, developed in a few short scenes, is enchantingly beautiful: an affecting union of chivalrous magnanimity on the one part, and on the other of the virgin openness of a heart which, brought up far from the world on an uninhabited island, has never learned to disguise its innocent movements. The wisdom of the princely hermit Prospero has a magical and mysterious air; the disagreeable impression left by the black falsehood of the two usurpers is softened by the honest gossipping of the old and faithful Gonzalo; Trinculo and Stephano, two good-for-nothing drunkards, find a worthy associate in Caliban; and Ariel hovers sweetly over the whole as the personified genius of the wonderful fable.

Caliban has become a by-word as the strange creation of a poetical imagination. A mixture of gnome and savage, half dæmon, half brute, in his behaviour we perceive at once the traces of his native disposition, and the influence of Prospero's education. The latter could only unfold his understanding, without, in the slightest degree, taming his rooted malignity: it is as if the use of reason and human speech were communicated to an awkward ape. In inclination Caliban is malicious, cowardly, false, and base; and yet he is essentially different from the vulgar knaves of a civilized world, as portrayed occasionally by Shakespeare. He is rude, but not vulgar; he never falls into the prosaic and low familiarity of his drunken associates, for he is, in his way, a poetical being; he always speaks in verse. He has picked up every thing dissonant and thorny in language to compose out of it a vocabulary of his own; and of the whole variety of nature, the hateful, repulsive, and pettily deformed have alone been impressed on his imagination. The magical world of spirits, which the staff of Prospero has assembled on the island, casts merely a faint reflection into his mind, as a ray of light which falls into a dark cave, incapable of communicating to it either heat or illumination, serves merely to set in motion the poisonous vapours. The delineation of this monster is throughout inconceivably consistent and profound, and, notwithstanding its hatefulness, by no means hurtful to our feelings, as the honour of human nature is left untouched.

In the zephyr-like Ariel the image of air is not to be mistaken ; his name even bears an allusion to it ; as, on the other hand, Caliban signifies the heavy element of earth. Yet they are neither of them simple, allegorical personifications, but beings individually determined. In general we find in *The Midsummer Night's Dream*, in *The Tempest*, in the magical part of *Macbeth*, and wherever Shakespeare avails himself of the popular belief in the invisible presence of spirits, and the possibility of coming in contact with them, a profound view of the inward life of Nature and her mysterious springs, which, it is true, can never be altogether unknown to the genuine poet, as poetry is altogether incompatible with mechanical physics, but which few have possessed in an equal degree with Dante and himself.

[*From Mrs. Jameson's "Characteristics of Women."*]

We might have deemed it impossible to go beyond Viola, Perdita, and Ophelia as pictures of feminine beauty ; to exceed the one in tender delicacy, the other in ideal grace, and the last in simplicity, if Shakespeare had not done this ; and he alone could have done it. Had he never created a Miranda, we should never have been made to feel how completely the purely natural and the purely ideal can blend into each other.

The character of Miranda resolves itself into the very elements of womanhood. She is beautiful, modest, and tender, and she is these only ; they comprise her whole being, external and internal. She is so perfectly unsophisticated, so delicately refined, that she is all but ethereal. Let us imagine any other woman placed beside Miranda — even one of Shakespeare's own loveliest and sweetest creations—there is not one of them that could sustain the comparison for a moment; not one that would not appear somewhat coarse or artificial when brought into immediate contact with this pure child of nature, this "Eve of an enchanted Paradise."

What, then, has Shakespeare done?—"O wondrous skill and sweet wit of the man!"—he has removed Miranda far from all comparison with her own sex; he has placed her between the demi-demon of earth and the delicate spirit of air. The next step is into the ideal and supernatural; and the only being who approaches Miranda, with whom she can be contrasted, is Ariel. Beside the subtle essence of this ethereal sprite, this creature of elemental light and air, that "ran upon the winds, rode the curl'd clouds, and in the colours of the rainbow lived," Miranda herself appears a palpable reality, a woman, "breathing thoughtful breath," a woman, walking the earth in her mortal loveliness, with a heart as frail-strung, as passion-touched, as ever fluttered in a female bosom.

I have said that Miranda possesses merely the elementary attributes of womanhood, but each of these stands in her with a distinct and peculiar grace. She resembles nothing upon earth; but do we therefore compare her, in our own minds, with any of those fabled beings with which the fancy of ancient poets peopled the forest depths, the fountain or the ocean?—oread or dryad fleet, sea-maid, or naiad of the stream? We cannot think of them together. Miranda is a consistent, natural human being. Our impression of her nymph-like beauty, her peerless grace, and purity of soul, has a distinct and individual character. Not only is she exquisitely lovely, being what she is, but we are made to feel that she *could* not possibly be otherwise than as she is portrayed. She has never beheld one of her own sex; she has never caught from society one imitated or artificial grace. The impulses which have come to her, in her enchanted solitude, are of heaven and nature, not of the world and its vanities. She has sprung up into beauty beneath the eye of her father, the princely magician; her companions have been the rocks and woods, the many-shaped, many-tinted clouds, and the silent stars; her playmates the ocean billows, that stooped their foamy crests, and ran rippling to kiss her feet. Ariel and his attendant sprites hovered over her head, ministered duteous to her every wish, and presented before her pageants of beauty and grandeur. The very air, made vocal by her father's art, floated in music around her. If we can presuppose such a situation with all its circumstances, do we not behold in the character of Miranda not only the credible, but the natural, the necessary results of such a situation? She retains her woman's heart, for that is unalterable and inalienable, as a part of her being; but her deportment, her looks, her language, her thoughts—all these, from the supernatural and poetical circumstances around her, assume a cast of the pure ideal; and to us, who are in the secret of her human and pitying nature, nothing can be more charming and consistent than the effect which she produces upon others, who, never having beheld any thing resembling her, approach her as "a wonder," as something celestial:—

> Most sure, the goddess on whom these airs attend!

And again:—

> What is this maid?
> Is she the goddess who hath severed us,
> And brought us thus together?

Contrasted with the impression of her refined and dignified beauty, and its effect on all beholders, is Miranda's own soft simplicity, her virgin innocence, her total ignorance of the conventional forms and language of society. It is most natural that in a being thus constituted, the first tears should spring from compassion, "suffering with those that she saw suffer;" and that her first sigh should be offered to a love at once fearless and submissive, delicate and fond. She has no taught scruples of honour like Juliet; no coy concealments like Viola; no assumed dignity standing in its own defence. Her bashfulness is less a quality than an instinct; it is like the self-folding of a flower, spontaneous and unconscious. I suppose there is nothing of the kind in poetry equal to the scene between Ferdinand and Miranda. In Ferdinand, who is a noble creature, we have all the chivalrous magnanimity with which man, in a high state of civilization, disguises his real superiority, and does humble homage to the being of whose destiny he disposes; while Miranda, the mere child of nature, is struck with wonder at her own new emotions. Only conscious of her own weakness as a woman, and ignorant of those usages of society which teach us to dissemble the real passion, and assume (and sometimes abuse) an unreal and transient power, she is equally ready to place her life, her love, her service beneath his feet. . . .

As Miranda, being what she is, could only have had a Ferdinand for a lover, and an Ariel for her attendant, so she could have had with propriety no other father than the majestic and gifted being who fondly claims her as "a thread of his own life—nay, that for which he lives." Prospero, with his magical powers, his superhuman wisdom, his moral worth and grandeur, and his kingly dignity, is one of the most sublime visions that ever swept with ample robes, pale brow, and sceptred hand, before the eye of fancy. He controls the invisible world, and works through the agency of spirits; not by any evil and forbidden compact, but solely by superior might of intellect—by potent spells gathered from the lore of ages, and abjured when he mingles again as a man with his fellow-men. He is as distinct a being from the necromancers and astrologers celebrated in Shakespeare's age as can well be imagined:* and all the wizards of poetry and fiction, even

* Such as Cornelius Agrippa, Michael Scott, Dr. Dee. The last was the contemporary of Shakespeare.

Faust and St. Leon, sink into commonplaces before the princely, the philosophic, the benevolent Prospero.

[*From Hazlitt's "Characters of Shakespeare's Plays."**]

*The Tempest* is one of the most original and perfect of Shakespeare's productions, and he has shown in it all the variety of his powers. It is full of grace and grandeur. The human and imaginary characters, the dramatic and the grotesque, are blended together with the greatest art, and without any appearance of it. Though he has here given "to airy nothing a local habitation and a name," yet that part which is only the fantastic creation of his mind has the same palpable texture, and coheres "semblably" with the rest. As the preternatural part has the air of reality, and almost haunts the imagination with a sense of truth, the real characters and events partake of the wildness of a dream. The stately magician Prospero, driven from his dukedom, but around whom (so potent is his art) airy spirits throng numberless to do his bidding; his daughter Miranda ("worthy of that name"), to whom all the power of his art points, and who seems the goddess of the isle; the princely Ferdinand, cast by fate upon the haven of his happiness in this idol of his love; the delicate Ariel; the savage Caliban, half brute, half demon; the drunken ship's crew—are all connected parts of the story, and can hardly be spared from the place they fill. Even the local scenery is of a piece and character with the subject. Prospero's enchanted island seems to have risen up out of the sea; the airy music, the tempest-tossed vessel, the turbulent waves, all have the effect of the landscape background of some fine picture. Shakespeare's pencil is (to use an allusion of his own) "like the dyer's hand, subdued to what it works in." Everything in him, though it partakes of "the liberty of wit," is also subjected to "the law" of the understanding. For instance, even the drunken sailors, who are made

* Edited by Wm. Carew Hazlitt, London, 1869, p. 82 foll.

reeling ripe, share, in the disorder of their minds and bodies, in the tumult of the elements, and seem on shore to be as much at the mercy of chance as they were before at the mercy of the wind and waves. These fellows with their sea-wit are the least to our taste of any part of the play; but they are as like drunken sailors as they can be, and are an indirect foil to Caliban, whose figure acquires a classical dignity in the comparison.

The character of Caliban is generally thought (and justly so) to be one of the author's masterpieces. It is not indeed pleasant to see this character on the stage, any more than it is to see the god Pan personated there. But in itself it is one of the wildest and most abstracted of all Shakespeare's characters, whose deformity, whether of body or mind, is redeemed by the power and truth of the imagination displayed in it. It is the essence of grossness, but there is not a particle of vulgarity in it. Shakespeare has described the brutal mind of Caliban in contact with the pure and original forms of nature; the character grows out of the soil where it is rooted, uncontrolled, uncouth, and wild, uncramped by any of the meannesses of custom. It is "of the earth, earthy." It seems almost to have been dug out of the ground, with a soul instinctively superadded to it answering to its wants and origin. Vulgarity is not natural coarseness, but conventional coarseness, learned from others, contrary to, or without an entire conformity of natural power and disposition; as fashion is the commonplace affectation of what is elegant and refined without any feeling of the essence of it. Schlegel, the admirable German critic of Shakespeare, observes that Caliban is a poetical character, and "always speaks in blank verse." . . . .

In conducting Stephano and Trinculo to Prospero's cell, Caliban shows the superiority of natural capacity over greater knowedge and greater folly; and in a former scene, when Ariel frightens them with his music, Caliban, to encourage them, accounts for it in the eloquent poetry of the senses:

Be not afeard; the isle is full of noises,
Sounds and sweet airs, that give delight and hurt not.
Sometimes a thousand twangling instruments
Will hum about mine ears; and sometimes voices,
That, if I then had wak'd after long sleep,
Will make me sleep again: and then, in dreaming,
The clouds, methought, would open, and show riches
Ready to drop upon me; that when I wak'd
I cried to dream again.

This is not more beautiful than it is true. The poet here shows us the savage with the simplicity of a child. Shakespeare had to paint the human animal rude and without choice in its pleasures, but not without the sense of pleasure or some germ of the affections. Master Barnardine, in *Measure for Measure*, the savage of civilized life, is an admirable philosophical counterpart to Caliban.

Shakespeare has, as it were by design, drawn off from Caliban the elements of whatever is ethereal and refined, to compound them in the unearthly mould of Ariel. Nothing was ever more finely conceived than this contrast between the material and the spiritual, the gross and delicate. Ariel is imaginary power, the swiftness of thought personified. When told to make good speed by Prospero, he says, "I drink the air before me." This is something like Puck's boast on a similar occasion, "I'll put a girdle round about the earth in forty minutes." But Ariel differs from Puck in having a fellow-feeling in the interests of those he is employed about. How requisite is the following dialogue between him and Prospero!

*Ariel.* Your charm so strongly works them,
That if you now beheld them, your affections
Would become tender.
*Prospero.* Dost thou think so, spirit?
*Ariel.* Mine would, sir, were I human.
*Prospero.* And mine shall.
Hast thou, which art but air, a touch, a feeling
Of their afflictions, and shall not myself,

One of their kind, that relish all as sharply
Passion as they, be kindlier moved than thou art?

It has been observed that there is a peculiar charm in the songs introduced in Shakespeare, which, without conveying any distinct images, seem to recall all the feelings connected with them, like snatches of half-forgotten music heard indistinctly and at intervals. There is this effect produced by Ariel's songs, which (as we are told) seem to sound in the air, and as if the person playing them were invisible.

[*From Franz Horn's "Shakespeare's Schauspiele Erlautert.*"*]

In Prospero we have a delineation of peculiar profundity. He was once not altogether a just prince, not thoroughly a just man; but he had the disposition to be both. His soul thirsted after knowledge; his mind, sincere in itself, after love; and his fancy, after the secrets of nature; but he forgot, what a prince should least of all forget, that, upon this moving earth, superior acquirements, in order to stand firmly, must be exercised carefully; that the world is full of enemies who can only be subdued by a watchful power and prudence, and that in certain situations the armour ought never to be put off. Thus it became easy for his nearest relation, his brother, with the help of a powerful neighbouring king who could not resist the offered but unjustifiable advantage, to depose him from his dukedom. But as the pure morals of the prince, although they were perhaps but lazily exercised in behalf of his subjects, had nevertheless gained him their love, and the usurper did not dare to make an attack on the lives of the fallen, Prospero saved himself, his daughter, and a part of his magical books, upon a desert island. Here he becomes, what, in its highest sense, he had not yet been, a father and prince. His knowledge extends. Nature listens to him, perhaps because he learned to know and love her more inwardly. Zephyr-like spirits, full of a tender frolicsome humour,

* Knight's translation, with a few verbal changes.

and rude earth-born gnomes, are compelled to serve him. The whole island is full of wonders, but only such as the fancy willingly receives, of sounds and songs, of merry helpers and comical tormentors; and Prospero shows his great human wisdom particularly in the manner with which he, as the spiritual centre, knows how to conduct his intercourse with friends and foes. . . .

In Caliban there is a curious mixture of devil, man, and beast. He desires evil, not for the sake of evil or from mere wickedness, but because it is *piquant*, and because he feels himself oppressed. He is convinced that gross injustice has been done him, and thus he does not rightly feel that what he desires may be wicked. He knows perfectly well how powerful Prospero is, whose art may perhaps even subdue his maternal god Setebos, and that he himself is unfortunately nothing but a slave. Nevertheless, he cannot cease to curse, and certainly with the gusto of a virtuoso in this more than liberal art. Whatever he can find most base and disgusting he surrounds almost artistically with the most inharmonious murmuring and hissing words, and then wishes them to fall upon Prospero and his lovely daughter. He knows very well that all this will help him nothing, but that at night he will have "cramps," and "side-stitches," and be "pinched by urchins," but still he continues to pour out new curses. He has acquired one fixed idea—that the island belonged to his mother, and, consequently, now to himself, the crown prince. The greatest horrors are pleasant to him, for he feels them only as jests which break the monotony of his slavery. He laments that he had been prevented from completing a frightful sin, "Would it had been done," etc.; and the thought of a murder gives him a real enjoyment, perhaps chiefly on account of the noise and confusion that it would produce.

Recognizing all this, yet our feelings towards him never rise to a thorough hatred. We find him only laughably horrible, and as a marvellous, though at bottom a feeble monster, highly interesting, for we foresee from the first that none of his threats will be fulfilled. Caliban could scarcely at any time have been made out more in detail, but we are well enabled to seize upon the idea of his inner physiognomy from the naked sketch of his external form. He is, with all his foolish rage and wickedness, not entirely vulgar; and though he allows himself to be imposed upon, even by his miserable comrades (perhaps only because they are men, and, if ugly, yet handsomer than himself), he everywhere shows more prudence, which is only checked because he considers himself more powerful than he really is. Indeed, he stands far higher than Trinculo and Stephano.

Opposed to him stands Ariel, by no means an ethereal, featureless angel, but as a real airy and frolicsome spirit, agreeable and open, but also capricious, roguish, and, with his other qualities, somewhat mischievous. He is thankful to Prospero for his release from the most confined of all confined situations, but his gratitude is not a natural virtue (we might almost add, not an airy virtue); therefore he must (like man) be sometimes reminded of his debt, and held in check. Only the promise of his freedom in two days restores him again to his amiability, and he then finds pleasure in executing the plans of his master with a delightful activity.

We noticed in passing "the featureless angel," and it requires no further indication where to find such beings; for no one will deny that these immortal winged children (so charming in many old German pictures), with their somewhat dull immortal harps, and, if possible, their still more dull and immortal anthems cause a not less immortal tediousness in the works of many poets. Shakespeare did not fall into this error, and it is in the highest degree attractive to observe the various and safe modes in which he manages the marvellous. In the storm he achieves his object by the simplest means, while, as has been already indicated, he represents Nature herself, and certainly justly, as the greatest miracle. When he has once in his own gentle way led us to believe that Prospero, through his high art, is able to overrule Nature—and how willingly do we believe in these higher powers of man !—how completely natural, and, to a certain degree, what merely pleasant trifles, are all the wonders which we see playing around us ! These higher powers, also, are not confined to Prospero alone ; Ferdinand and Miranda have, without any enchanted wand or any prolix instruction, full superiority over the wonders of nature, and they allow them to pass around them merely as a delightful drama ; for the highest wonder is in their own breasts—love, the pure human, and even on that account holy, love.

Even the pure mind and the firm heart, as they are shown in old Gonzalo, are armed with an almost similar power. With our poet, a truly moral man is always amiable, powerful, agreeable, and quietly wards off the snares laid for him. This old Gonzalo is so entirely occupied with his duty, in which alone he finds his pleasure, that he scarcely notices the gnat-stings of wit with which his opponents persecute him ; or, if he observes, easily and firmly repels them. What wit indeed has he to fear, who, in a sinking ship, has power remaining to sustain himself and others with genuine humour? Shakespeare seems scarcely to recognize a powerless virtue, and he depicts it only in cases of need ; so everything closes satisfactorily. The pure poetry of nature and genius inspires us ; and when we hear Prospero recite his far too modest epilogue, after laying down his enchanted wand, we have no wish to turn our minds to any frivolous thoughts, for the magic we have experienced was too charming and too mighty not to be enduring.

[*From Verplanck's Introduction to the Play.*]

*The Tempest* is one of those works for which no other production of the author's prolific fancy could have prepared his readers. It is wholly of a different cast of temper, and mood of disposition, from those so conspicuous in his gayer comedies; while even the ethical dignity and poetic splendour of *The Merchant of Venice* could not well lead the critic to anticipate the solemn grandeur, the unrivalled harmony and grace, the bold originality, and the grave beauty of *The Tempest*. . .

There are several respects in which the play thus stands alone as distinguishable in character from any other of its author's varied creations. Without being his work of greatest power, not equalling several other of the dramas in depth of passion, or in the exhibition of the working of the affections; surpassed by others in brilliancy of poetic fancy or exquisite delicacies of expression, it is nevertheless among the most perfect (perhaps, in fact, the most perfect) of all, as a work of art, of the most unbroken unity of effect and sustained majesty of intellect. It is, too—if we can speak of degrees of originality in the productions of this most creative of all poets—the most purely original of his conceptions, deriving nothing of any consequence from any other source for the plot, and without any prototype in literature of the more important personages, or any model for the thoughts and language, beyond the materials presented by actual and living human nature, to be raised and idealized into the "wild and wondrous" forms of Ariel and Caliban, of the majestic Prospero, and, above all, of his peerless daughter. Miranda is a character blending the truth of nature with the most exquisite refinement of poetic fancy, unrivalled even in Shakespeare's own long and beautiful series of portraitures of feminine excellence, and paralleled only by the Eve of Milton, who, I cannot but think, was indirectly indebted for some of her most fascinating attributes to the solitary daughter of Prospero.

Caliban, a being without example or parallel in poetic invention, degraded in mind, as well as in moral affections, below the level of humanity, and yet essentially and purely poetical in all his conceptions and language, is a creation to whose originality and poetic truth every critic, from Dryden downward, has paid homage. Nor is it a less striking peculiarity that the only buffoon characters and dialogue in the drama are those of the sailors, who seem to be introduced for the single purpose of contrasting the grossness and lowness of civilized vice with the nobler forms of savage and untutored depravity.

It is partly on account of this perfect novelty of invention, and probably still more from the fairy and magical machinery of the plot, that the later critics have designated *The Tempest* as specially belonging to the Romantic Drama. Yet to me it appears, not only in its structure, but in its taste and feeling, to bear a more classical character, and to be more assimilated to the higher Grecian drama, in its spirit, than any other of its author's works, or indeed any other poem of his age. The rules of the Greek stage, as to the unities of time and place, are fully complied with. This cannot well be the result of accident, for in an age of classical translation, and learned (even pedantic) imitation, it needed no classical learning to make the unities known to any dramatic author; and as Shakespeare had, in his other plays, totally rejected them, he would seem here to have expressly designed to conform his plot to their laws. But there also appears to me to be something in the poetic character and tone of the drama, approaching to the spirit and manner of the Greek dramatic poetry, which can certainly not be ascribed to intentional imitation, any more than to the unconscious resemblance often produced by habitual familiarity with favourite models. It has nothing of the air of learned and elaborate imitation which, in the works of Tasso, and Milton, and Gray, make the scholar everywhere as perceptible as the poet. But it is the resemblance of solemn thought, of calm dignity, of moral wisdom, of the dramatic dialogue in its most majestic form, passing now into the lyrical and now into the didactic or ethical. This resemblance of taste and feeling is rendered more striking by a similar bold and free invention and combination of poetic diction, making the English language as flexible as the Greek to every shade of thought. In all these respects, the resemblance to antiquity goes just far enough to show that its result is not artificial or intentional, but the result of the same mental causes operating upon the author's poetic temperament and taste at the time, which predominated in forming the "lofty grave tragedians" of ancient Athens.

ARIEL AS A SEA-NYMPH.

NAPLES.

# THE TEMPEST.

## *DRAMATIS PERSONÆ.*

ALONSO, King of Naples.
SEBASTIAN, his brother.
PROSPERO, the right Duke of Milan.
ANTONIO, his brother, the usurping Duke of Milan.
FERDINAND, son to the King of Naples.
GONZALO, an honest old Counsellor.
ADRIAN, FRANCISCO, } Lords
CALIBAN, a savage and deformed Slave.
TRINCULO, a Jester.
STEPHANO, a drunken Butler.

Master of a Ship, Boatswain, Mariners.
MIRANDA, daughter to Prospero.
ARIEL, an airy Spirit.
IRIS, CERES, JUNO, Nymphs, Reapers, } presented by Spirits.
Other Spirits attending on Prospero.

SCENE: *A ship at sea: an uninhabited island.*

## ACT I.

SCENE I. *On a ship at sea: a tempestuous noise of thunder and lightning heard.*

*Enter* a Ship-master *and* a Boatswain.

*Master.* Boatswain!

*Boatswain.* Here, master: what cheer?

*Master.* Good, speak to th' mariners: fall to't, yarely, or we run ourselves aground: bestir, bestir. [*Exit.*

*Enter* Mariners.

*Boatswain.* Heigh, my hearts! cheerly, cheerly, my hearts! yare, yare! Take in the topsail. Tend to th' master's whistle. Blow till thou burst thy wind, if room enough!

*Enter* ALONSO, SEBASTIAN, ANTONIO, FERDINAND, GONZALO, *and others.*

*Alonso.* Good boatswain, have care. Where's the master? Play the men.

*Boatswain.* I pray now, keep below.

*Antonio.* Where is the master, boatswain?

*Boatswain.* Do you not hear him? You mar our labour. Keep your cabins; you do assist the storm.

*Gonzalo.* Nay, good, be patient.

*Boatswain.* When the sea is. Hence! What cares these roarers for the name of king? To cabin! Silence! trouble us not.

*Gonzalo.* Good, yet remember whom thou hast aboard.

*Boatswain.* None that I love more than myself. You are a Counsellor; if you can command these elements to silence, and work the peace of the present, we will not hand a rope more. Use your authority: if you cannot, give thanks you have liv'd so long, and make yourself ready in your cabin for the mischance of the hour, if it so hap.—Cheerly, good hearts!—Out of our way, I say. [*Exit.*

*Gonzalo.* I have great comfort from this fellow: methinks he hath no drowning mark upon him; his complexion is perfect gallows. Stand fast, good Fate, to his hanging! Make the rope of his destiny our cable, for our own doth little advantage! If he be not born to be hang'd, our case is miserable. [*Exeunt.*

*Enter* Boatswain.

*Boatswain.* Down with the topmast! yare! lower, lower!

Bring her to try wi' th' main-course. [*A cry within.*] A plague upon this howling! they are louder than the weather or our office.—

*Enter* SEBASTIAN, ANTONIO, *and* GONZALO.

Yet again! what do you here? Shall we give o'er, and drown? Have you a mind to sink?

*Sebastian.* A plague o' your throat, you bawling, blasphemous, incharitable dog!

*Boatswain.* Work you, then.

*Antonio.* Hang, cur! hang, you whoreson, insolent noisemaker! We are less afraid to be drown'd than thou art.

*Gonzalo.* I'll warrant him for drowning, though the ship were no stronger than a nutshell.

*Boatswain.* Lay her a-hold, a-hold! Set her two courses. Off to sea again: lay her off.

*Enter* Mariners *wet.*

*Mariners.* All lost! to prayers, to prayers! all lost

*Boatswain.* What! must our mouths be cold?

*Gonzalo.* The king and prince at prayers! Let's assist them,
For our case is as theirs.

*Sebastian.* I'm out of patience.

*Antonio.* We are merely cheated of our lives by drunkards.—
This wide-chapp'd rascal,—would thou mightst lie drowning
The washing of ten tides!

*Gonzalo.* He'll be hang'd yet,
Though every drop of water swear against it,
And gape at wid'st to glut him.

[*A confused noise within.* "Mercy on us!"—
"We split, we split!"—"Farewell, my wife and children!"—
"Farewell, brother!"—"We split, we split, we split!"—]

*Antonio.* Let's all sink wi' th' king. [*Exit.*

*Sebastian.* Let's take leave of him. [*Exit.*

*Gonzalo.* Now would I give a thousand furlongs of sea for an acre of barren ground; long heath, brown furze, any thing. The wills above be done! but I would fain die a dry death. [*Exit.*

SCENE II. *The island. Before* PROSPERO'S *cell.*

*Enter* PROSPERO *and* MIRANDA.

*Miranda.* If by your art, my dearest father, you have
Put the wild waters in this roar, allay them.
The sky, it seems, would pour down stinking pitch,
But that the sea, mounting to th' welkin's cheek,
Dashes the fire out. O, I have suffered
With those that I saw suffer! A brave vessel,
Who had, no doubt, some noble creature in her,
Dash'd all to pieces. O, the cry did knock
Against my very heart! Poor souls, they perish'd!
Had I been any god of power, I would
Have sunk the sea within the earth, or ere
It should the good ship so have swallow'd and
The fraughting souls within her.

*Prospero.* Be collected:
No more amazement. Tell your piteous heart
There's no harm done.

*Miranda.* O, woe the day!

*Prospero.* No harm.
I have done nothing but in care of thee
(Of thee, my dear one! thee, my daughter!), who
Art ignorant of what thou art, naught knowing
Of whence I am, nor that I am more better
Than Prospero, master of a full poor cell,
And thy no greater father.

*Miranda.* More to know
Did never meddle with my thoughts.

*Prospero.* 'Tis time

I should inform thee farther. Lend thy hand,
And pluck my magic garment from me.—So :
[*Lays down his mantle.*
Lie there, my art.—Wipe thou thine eyes ; have comfort.
The direful spectacle of the wrack, which touch'd
The very virtue of compassion in thee,
I have with such provision in mine art
So safely order'd, that there is no soul—
No, not so much perdition as an hair
Betid to any creature in the vessel
Which thou heard'st cry, which thou saw'st sink. Sit down ;
For thou must now know farther.

*Miranda.* You have often
Begun to tell me what I am ; but stopp'd,
And left me to a bootless inquisition,
Concluding,—" Stay, not yet."

*Prospero.* The hour's now come ;
The very minute bids thee ope thine ear :
Obey, and be attentive. Canst thou remember
A time before we came unto this cell ?
I do not think thou canst ; for then thou wast not
Out three years old.

*Miranda.* Certainly, sir, I can.

*Prospero.* By what ? by any other house or person ?
Of any thing the image tell me that
Hath kept with thy remembrance.

*Miranda.* 'Tis far off,
And rather like a dream than an assurance
That my remembrance warrants. Had I not
Four or five women once that tended me ?

*Prospero.* Thou hadst, and more, Miranda. But how is it
That this lives in thy mind ? What seest thou else
In the dark backward and abysm of time ?
If thou remember'st aught ere thou cam'st here,
How thou cam'st here thou mayst.

*Miranda.* But that I do not.
*Prospero.* Twelve year since, Miranda, twelve year since,
Thy father was the Duke of Milan and
A prince of power.
*Miranda.* Sir, are not you my father?
*Prospero.* Thy mother was a piece of virtue, and
She said thou wast my daughter; and thy father
Was Duke of Milan; and his only heir
And princess, no worse issued.
*Miranda.* O the heavens!
What foul play had we, that we came from thence?
Or blessed was't we did?
*Prospero.* Both, both, my girl:
By foul play, as thou say'st, were we heav'd thence;
But blessedly holp hither.
*Miranda.* O, my heart bleeds
To think o' th' teen that I have turn'd you to,
Which is from my remembrance! Please you, farther.
*Prospero.* My brother, and thy uncle, call'd Antonio,—
I pray thee, mark me,—that a brother should
Be so perfidious!—he whom, next thyself,
Of all the world I lov'd, and to him put
The manage of my State; as at that time
Through all the signiories it was the first
(And Prospero the prime duke, being so reputed
In dignity), and, for the liberal arts,
Without a parallel; those being all my study,
The government I cast upon my brother,
And to my State grew stranger, being transported
And rapt in secret studies. Thy false uncle—
Dost thou attend me?
*Miranda.* Sir, most heedfully.
*Prospero.* Being once perfected how to grant suits,
How to deny them, who t' advance, and who
To trash for over-topping, new created

The creatures that were mine, I say, or chang'd 'em,
Or else new form'd 'em; having both the key
Of officer and office, set all hearts i' th' State
To what tune pleas'd his ear, that now he was
The ivy which had hid my princely trunk,
And suck'd my verdure out on't.—Thou attend'st not.

*Miranda.* O, good sir, I do!

*Prospero.* I pray thee, mark me.
I, thus neglecting worldly ends, all dedicated
To closeness and the bettering of my mind
With that which, but by being so retir'd,
O'er-priz'd all popular rate, in my false brother
Awak'd an evil nature; and my trust,
Like a good parent, did beget of him
A falsehood, in its contrary as great
As my trust was; which had indeed no limit,
A confidence sans bound. He being thus lorded,
Not only with what my revenue yielded,
But what my power might else exact—like one
Who having unto truth, by telling of it,
Made such a sinner of his memory,
To credit his own lie—he did believe
He was indeed the duke, out o' th' substitution,
And executing th' outward face of royalty,
With all prerogative:—hence his ambition
Growing,—dost thou hear?

*Miranda.* Your tale, sir, would cure deafness.

*Prospero.* To have no screen between this part he play'd
And him he play'd it for, he needs will be
Absolute Milan. Me, poor man!—my library
Was dukedom large enough. Of temporal royalties
He thinks me now incapable; confederates
(So dry he was for sway) wi' th' King of Naples
To give him annual tribute, do him homage,
Subject his coronet to his crown, and bend

The dukedom, yet unbow'd (alas, poor Milan!),
To most ignoble stooping.
*Miranda.* O the heavens!
*Prospero.* Mark his condition, and th' event; then tell me
If this might be a brother.
*Miranda.* I should sin
To think but nobly of my grandmother:
Good wombs have borne bad sons.
*Prospero.* Now the condition.
This King of Naples, being an enemy
To me inveterate, hearkens my brother's suit;
Which was, that he, in lieu o' th' premises,
Of homage and I know not how much tribute,
Should presently extirpate me and mine
Out of the dukedom, and confer fair Milan,
With all the honours, on my brother: whereon,
A treacherous army levied, one midnight
Fated to th' purpose, did Antonio open
The gates of Milan; and, i' th' dead of darkness,
The ministers for th' purpose hurried thence
Me and thy crying self.
*Miranda.* Alack, for pity!
I, not remembering how I cried out then,
Will cry it o'er again: it is a hint
That wrings mine eyes to't.
*Prospero.* Hear a little further,
And then I'll bring thee to the present business
Which now's upon 's; without the which this story
Were most impertinent.
*Miranda.* Wherefore did they not
That hour destroy us?
*Prospero.* Well demanded, wench:
My tale provokes that question. Dear, they durst not,
So dear the love my people bore me; nor set
A mark so bloody on the business, but

With colors fairer painted their foul ends.
In few, they hurried us aboard a bark,
Bore us some leagues to sea; where they prepar'd
A rotten carcass of a boat, not rigg'd,
Nor tackle, sail, nor mast; the very rats
Instinctively have quit it. There they hoist us,
To cry to th' sea that roar'd to us; to sigh
To th' winds, whose pity, sighing back again,
Did us but loving wrong.

*Miranda.* Alack, what trouble
Was I then to you!

*Prospero.* O, a cherubin
Thou wast, that did preserve me. Thou did'st smile,
Infused with a fortitude from heaven,
When I have deck'd the sea with drops full salt,
Under my burthen groan'd; which rais'd in me
An undergoing stomach, to bear up
Against what should ensue.

*Miranda.* How came we ashore?

*Prospero.* By Providence divine.
Some food we had, and some fresh water, that
A noble Neapolitan, Gonzalo,
Out of his charity (who being then appointed
Master of this design), did give us, with
Rich garments, linens, stuffs, and necessaries,
Which since have steaded much. So, of his gentleness,
Knowing I lov'd my books, he furnish'd me,
From mine own library, with volumes that
I prize above my dukedom.

*Miranda.* Would I might
But ever see that man!

*Prospero.* Now I arise:—
Sit still, and hear the last of our sea-sorrow.
Here in this island we arriv'd; and here
Have I, thy schoolmaster, made thee more profit

Than other princess can, that have more time
For vainer hours, and tutors not so careful.
*Miranda.* Heavens thank you for't! And now, I pray you, sir,
(For still 'tis beating in my mind,) your reason
For raising this sea-storm?
*Prospero.* Know thus far forth:
By accident most strange, bountiful Fortune
(Now my dear lady) hath mine enemies
Brought to this shore; and by my prescience
I find my zenith doth depend upon
A most auspicious star, whose influence
If now I court not, but omit, my fortunes
Will ever after droop. Here cease more questions:
Thou art inclin'd to sleep; 'tis a good dulness,
And give it way:—I know thou canst not choose.—
[*Miranda sleeps.*
Come away, servant, come! I am ready now:
Approach, my Ariel, come!

*Enter* ARIEL.

*Ariel.* All hail, great master! grave sir, hail! I come
To answer thy best pleasure; be't to fly,
To swim, to dive into the fire, to ride
On the curl'd clouds: to thy strong bidding task
Ariel and all his quality.
*Prospero.* Hast thou, spirit,
Perform'd to point the tempest that I bade thee?
*Ariel.* To every article.
I boarded the king's ship; now on the beak,
Now in the waist, the deck, in every cabin,
I flam'd amazement: sometime I'd divide,
And burn in many places; on the topmast,
The yards, and bowsprit, would I flame distinctly,
Then meet and join. Jove's lightnings, the precursors

O' th' dreadful thunder-claps, more momentary
And sight-outrunning were not: the fire and cracks
Of sulphurous roaring the most mighty Neptune
Seem to besiege, and make his bold waves tremble,
Yea, his dread trident shake.

*Prospero.* My brave spirit!
Who was so firm, so constant, that this coil
Would not infect his reason?

*Ariel.* Not a soul
But felt a fever of the mad, and play'd
Some tricks of desperation. All but mariners
Plung'd in the foaming brine, and quit the vessel,
Then all afire with me: the king's son, Ferdinand,
With hair up-staring,—then like reeds, not hair,—
Was the first man that leap'd; cried, "Hell is empty,
And all the devils are here."

*Prospero.* Why, that's my spirit!
But was not this nigh shore?

*Ariel.* Close by, my master.

*Prospero.* But are they, Ariel, safe?

*Ariel.* Not a hair perish'd;
On their sustaining garments not a blemish,
But fresher than before: and, as thou bad'st me,
In troops I have dispers'd them 'bout the isle.
The king's son have I landed by himself;
Whom I left cooling of the air with sighs
In an odd angle of the isle, and sitting,
His arms in this sad knot.

*Prospero.* Of the king's ship
The mariners, say how thou hast dispos'd,
And all the rest o' th' fleet.

*Ariel.* Safely in harbour
Is the king's ship; in the deep nook, where once
Thou call'dst me up at midnight to fetch dew
From the still-vex'd Bermoothes, there she's hid;

The mariners all under hatches stow'd;
Who, with a charm join'd to their suffer'd labour,
I have left asleep: and for the rest o' th' fleet,
Which I dispers'd, they all have met again,
And are upon the Mediterranean flote,
Bound sadly home for Naples,
Supposing that they saw the king's ship wrack'd,
And his great person perish.
*Prospero.* Ariel, thy charge
Exactly is perform'd; but there's more work.
What is the time o' th' day?
*Ariel.* Past the mid season.
*Prospero.* At least two glasses. The time 'twixt six and now
Must by us both be spent most preciously.
*Ariel.* Is there more toil? Since thou dost give me pains,
Let me remember thee what thou hast promis'd,
Which is not yet perform'd me.
*Prospero.* How now? moody?
What is't thou canst demand?
*Ariel.* My liberty.
*Prospero.* Before the time be out? no more!
*Ariel.* I prithee,
Remember I have done thee worthy service;
Told thee no lies, made no mistakings, serv'd
Without or grudge or grumblings. Thou didst promise
To bate me a full year
*Prospero.* Dost thou forget
From what a torment I did free thee?
*Ariel.* No.
*Prospero.* Thou dost; and think'st it much to tread the ooze
Of the salt deep,
To run upon the sharp wind of the north,
To do me business in the veins o' th' earth
When it is bak'd with frost.

*Ariel.* I do not, sir.

*Prospero.* Thou liest, malignant thing! Hast thou forgot
The foul witch Sycorax, who with age and envy
Was grown into a hoop? hast thou forgot her?

*Ariel.* No, sir.

*Prospero.* Thou hast. Where was she born? speak; [tell me.

*Ariel.* Sir, in Argier.

*Prospero.* O, was she so? I must
Once in a month recount what thou hast been,
Which thou forget'st. This damn'd witch Sycorax,
For mischiefs manifold, and sorceries terrible
To enter human hearing, from Argier,
Thou know'st, was banish'd: for one thing she did,
They would not take her life. Is not this true?

*Ariel.* Ay, sir.

*Prospero.* This blue-eyed hag was hither brought with child,
And here was left by th' sailors. Thou, my slave,
As thou report'st thyself, wast then her servant;
And, for thou wast a spirit too delicate
To act her earthy and abhorr'd commands,
Refusing her grand hests, she did confine thee,
By help of her more potent ministers,
And in her most unmitigable rage,
Into a cloven pine; within which rift
Imprison'd, thou didst painfully remain
A dozen years; within which space she died,
And left thee there, where thou didst vent thy groans
As fast as mill-wheels strike. Then was this island—
Save for the son that she did litter here,
A freckled whelp, hag-born—not honour'd with
A human shape.

*Ariel.* Yes, Caliban her son.

*Prospero.* Dull thing, I say so; he, that Caliban,
Whom now I keep in service. Thou best know'st
What torment I did find thee in; thy groans

Did make wolves howl, and penetrate the breasts
Of ever-angry bears. It was a torment
To lay upon the damn'd, which Sycorax
Could not again undo: it was mine art,
When I arriv'd and heard thee, that made gape
The pine, and let thee out.

*Ariel.* I thank thee, master.

*Prospero.* If thou more murmur'st, I will rend an oak,
And peg thee in his knotty entrails till
Thou hast howl'd away twelve winters.

*Ariel.* Pardon, master;
I will be correspondent to command,
And do my spriting gently.

*Prospero.* Do so; and after two days
I will discharge thee.

*Ariel.* That's my noble master!
What shall I do? say what; what shall I do?

*Prospero.* Go make thyself like a nymph o' th' sea: be subject
To no sight but thine and mine; invisible
To every eyeball else. Go, take this shape,
And hither come in't: go, hence with diligence!—

[*Exit Ariel.*

Awake, dear heart, awake! thou hast slept well;
Awake!

*Miranda.* The strangeness of your story put
Heaviness in me.

*Prospero.* Shake it off. Come on;
We'll visit Caliban my slave, who never
Yields us kind answer.

*Miranda.* 'Tis a villain, sir,
I do not love to look on.

*Prospero.* But, as 'tis,
We cannot miss him: he does make our fire,
Fetch in our wood, and serves in offices

That profit us.—What, ho! slave! Caliban!
Thou earth, thou! speak.
*Caliban* [*within*]. There's wood enough within.
*Prospero.* Come forth, I say! there's other business for thee:
Come, thou tortoise! when?—

*Enter* ARIEL, *like a water-nymph.*

Fine apparition! My quaint Ariel,
Hark in thine ear.
*Ariel.* My lord, it shall be done. [*Exit.*
*Prospero.* Thou poisonous slave, come forth!

*Enter* CALIBAN.

*Caliban.* As wicked dew as e'er my mother brush'd
With raven's feather from unwholesome fen
Drop on you both! a south-west blow on ye,
And blister you all o'er!
*Prospero.* For this, be sure, to-night thou shalt have cramps,
Side-stitches that shall pen thy breath up; urchins
Shall, for that vast of night that they may work,
All exercise on thee; thou shalt be pinch'd
As thick as honeycomb, each pinch more stinging
Than bees that made 'em.
*Caliban.* I must eat my dinner.
This island's mine, by Sycorax my mother,
Which thou tak'st from me. When thou camest first,
Thou strok'dst me and mad'st much of me, wouldst give me
Water with berries in't, and teach me how
To name the bigger light, and how the less,
That burn by day and night: and then I lov'd thee,
And show'd thee all the qualities o' th' isle,
The fresh springs, brine-pits, barren place and fertile.
Cursed be I that did so! All the charms
Of Sycorax, toads, beetles, bats, light on you!
For I am all the subjects that you have,

Which first was mine own king; and here you sty me
In this hard rock, whiles you do keep from me
The rest o' th' island.

*Prospero.* Thou most lying slave,
Whom stripes may move, not kindness! I have us'd thee,
Filth as thou art, with human care; and lodg'd thee
In mine own cell, till thou didst seek to violate
The honour of my child.

*Caliban.* O ho, O ho! would 't had been done!
Thou didst prevent me; I had peopled else
This isle with Calibans.

*Prospero.* Abhorred slave,
Which any print of goodness wilt not take,
Being capable of all ill! I pitied thee,
Took pains to make thee speak, taught thee each hour
One thing or other: when thou didst not, savage,
Know thine own meaning, but wouldst gabble like
A thing most brutish, I endow'd thy purposes
With words that made them known. But thy vile race,
Though thou didst learn, had that in't which good natures
Could not abide to be with; therefore wast thou
Deservedly confin'd into this rock,
Who hadst deserv'd more than a prison.

*Caliban.* You taught me language; and my profit on't
Is, I know how to curse. The red plague rid you
For learning me your language!

*Prospero.* Hag-seed, hence!
Fetch us in fuel; and be quick, thou'rt best,
To answer other business. Shrug'st thou, malice?
If thou neglect'st, or dost unwillingly
What I command, I'll rack thee with old cramps,
Fill all thy bones with aches, make thee roar,
That beasts shall tremble at thy din.

*Caliban.* No, pray thee.
[*Aside.*] I must obey: his art is of such power,

It would control my dam's god, Setebos,
And make a vassal of him.

*Prospero.* So, slave ; hence ! [*Exit Caliban.*

*Enter* FERDINAND, *and* ARIEL *(invisible), playing and singing.*

ARIEL.—Song.

*Come unto these yellow sands,*
*And then take hands :*
*Curtsied when you have, and kiss'd*
*The wild waves whist,*
*Foot it featly here and there ;*
*And, sweet sprites, the burthen bear.*

Burthen [dispersedly]. *Hark, hark !*
*Bowgh-wawgh.*
*The watch-dogs bark :*
*Bowgh-wawgh.*

ARIEL. *Hark, hark ! I hear*
*The strain of strutting chanticleer*
*Cry, Cock-a-didle-dow.*

*Ferdinand.* Where should this music be? i' th' air or th' [earth?—
It sounds no more ;—and, sure, it waits upon
Some god o' th' island. Sitting on a bank,
Weeping again the king my father's wrack,
This music crept by me upon the waters,
Allaying both their fury and my passion
With it's sweet air : thence I have follow'd it,
Or it hath drawn me rather. But 'tis gone.—
No, it begins again.

ARIEL.—Song.

*Full fathom five thy father lies ;*
*Of his bones are coral made ;*
*Those are pearls that were his eyes :*
*Nothing of him that doth fade,*

*But doth suffer a sea-change*
*Into something rich and strange.*
*Sea-nymphs hourly ring his knell:*
[Burthen.] *Ding-dong.*
*Hark! now I hear them—Ding-dong, bell.*

*Ferdinand.* The ditty does remember my drown'd father.
This is no mortal business, nor no sound
That the earth owes.—I hear it now above me.
*Prospero.* The fringed curtains of thine eye advance,
And say what thou seest yond.
*Miranda.* What is't? a spirit?
Lord, how it looks about! Believe me, sir,
It carries a brave form. But 'tis a spirit.
*Prospero.* No, wench; it eats and sleeps and hath such [senses
As we have—such. This gallant which thou seest
Was in the wrack; and, but he's something stain'd
With grief, that's beauty's canker, thou mightst call him
A goodly person. He hath lost his fellows,
And strays about to find 'em.
*Miranda.* I might call him
A thing divine; for nothing natural
I ever saw so noble.
*Prospero* [*Aside*]. It goes on, I see,
As my soul prompts it.—Spirit, fine spirit! I'll free thee
Within two days for this.
*Ferdinand.* Most sure, the goddess
On whom these airs attend!—Vouchsafe my prayer
May know if you remain upon this island;
And that you will some good instruction give
How I may bear me here: my prime request,
Which I do last pronounce, is, O you wonder!
If you be maid or no?
*Miranda.* No wonder, sir;
But certainly a maid.

*Ferdinand.* My language! heavens!—
I am the best of them that speak this speech,
Were I but where 'tis spoken.
*Prospero.* How? the best?
What wert thou, if the King of Naples heard thee?
*Ferdinand.* A single thing, as I am now, that wonders
To hear thee speak of Naples. He does hear me;
And that he does I weep: myself am Naples,
Who with mine eyes, never since at ebb, beheld
The king my father wrack'd.
*Miranda.* Alack, for mercy!
*Ferdinand.* Yes, faith, and all his lords; the Duke of Milan
And his brave son being twain.
*Prospero* [*Aside*]. The Duke of Milan,
And his more braver daughter, could control thee,
If now 'twere fit to do't.—At the first sight
They have chang'd eyes.—Delicate Ariel,
I'll set thee free for this.—[*To him.*] A word, good sir;
I fear you have done yourself some wrong: a word.
*Miranda.* Why speaks my father so ungently? This
Is the third man that e'er I saw; the first
That e'er I sigh'd for; pity move my father
To be inclin'd my way!
*Ferdinand.* O, if a virgin,
And your affection not gone forth, I'll make you
The queen of Naples.
*Prospero.* Soft, sir! one word more.—
[*Aside.*] They are both in either's powers: but this swift business
I must uneasy make, lest too light winning
Make the prize light.—[*To him.*] One word more; I charge thee
That thou attend me. Thou dost here usurp
The name thou ow'st not; and hast put thyself
Upon this island as a spy, to win it
From me, the lord on't.

*Ferdinand.* No, as I am a man.
*Miranda.* There's nothing ill can dwell in such a temple:
If the ill spirit have so fair a house,
Good things will strive to dwell with't.
*Prospero.* [*To Ferdinand.*] Follow me.—
Speak not you for him; he's a traitor.—Come;
I'll manacle thy neck and feet together:
Sea-water shalt thou drink; thy food shall be
The fresh-brook muscles, wither'd roots, and husks
Wherein the acorn cradled. Follow.
*Ferdinand.* No;
I will resist such entertainment till
Mine enemy has more power.
[*He draws, and is charmed from moving.*
*Miranda.* O dear father!
Make not too rash a trial of him, for
He's gentle, and not fearful.
*Prospero.* What! I say,
My foot my tutor?—Put thy sword up, traitor;
Who mak'st a show, but dar'st not strike, thy conscience
Is so possess'd with guilt: come from thy ward;
For I can here disarm thee with this stick,
And make thy weapon drop.
*Miranda.* Beseech you, father!
*Prospero.* Hence! hang not on my garments.
*Miranda.* Sir, have pity;
I'll be his surety.
*Prospero.* Silence! one word more
Shall make me chide thee, if not hate thee. What!
An advocate for an impostor! hush!
Thou think'st there is no more such shapes as he,
Having seen but him and Caliban: foolish wench!
To th' most of men this is a Caliban,
And they to him are angels.
*Miranda.* My affections

Are, then, most humble ; I have no ambition
To see a goodlier man.

*Prospero.* [*To Ferdinand.*] Come on ; obey :
Thy nerves are in their infancy again,
And have no vigour in them.

*Ferdinand.* So they are :
My spirits, as in a dream, are all bound up.
My father's loss, the weakness which I feel,
The wrack of all my friends, nor this man's threats
To whom I am subdued, are but light to me,
Might I but through my prison once a day
Behold this maid. All corners else o' th' earth
Let liberty make use of; space enough
Have I in such a prison.

*Prospero* [*Aside*]. It works. [*To Ferdinand.*] Come on.—
Thou hast done well, fine Ariel !—Follow me.—
[*To Ariel.*] Hark what thou else shalt do me.

*Miranda.* Be of comfort.
My father's of a better nature, sir,
Than he appears by speech : this is unwonted
Which now came from him.

*Prospero.* Thou shalt be as free
As mountain winds : but then exactly do
All points of my command.

*Ariel.* To the syllable.

*Prospero.* Come, follow.—Speak not for him. [*Exeunt.*

## ACT II.

SCENE I. *Another part of the island.*

*Enter* ALONSO, SEBASTIAN, ANTONIO, GONZALO, ADRIAN, FRANCISCO, *and others.*

*Gonzalo.* Beseech you, sir, be merry; you have cause
(So have we all) of joy; for our escape
Is much beyond our loss. Our hint of woe
Is common: every day, some sailor's wife,

The masters of some merchant, and the merchant,
Have just our theme of woe; but for the miracle—
I mean our preservation—few in millions
Can speak like us: then wisely, good sir, weigh
Our sorrow with our comfort.

*Alonso.* Prithee, peace.

*Sebastian.* He receives comfort like cold porridge.

*Antonio.* The visitor will not give him o'er so.

*Sebastian.* Look, he's winding up the watch of his wit; by and by it will strike.

*Gonzalo.* Sir,—

*Sebastian.* One: tell.

*Gonzalo.* When every grief is entertain'd that's offer'd,
Comes to the entertainer—

*Sebastian.* A dollar.

*Gonzalo.* Dolour comes to him, indeed: you have spoken truer than you purpos'd.

*Sebastian.* You have taken it wiselier than I meant you should.

*Gonzalo.* Therefore, my lord,—

*Antonio.* Fie, what a spendthrift is he of his tongue!

*Alonso.* I prithee, spare.

*Gonzalo.* Well, I have done: but yet,—

*Sebastian.* He will be talking.

*Antonio.* Which, of he or Adrian, for a good wager, first begins to crow?

*Sebastian.* The old cock.

*Antonio.* The cockerel.

*Sebastian.* Done. The wager?

*Antonio.* A laughter.

*Sebastian.* A match!

*Adrian.* Though this island seem to be desert,—

*Antonio.* Ha, ha, ha!

*Sebastian.* So, you're paid.

*Adrian.* Uninhabitable, and almost inaccessible,—

*Sebastian.* Yet,—

*Adrian.* Yet,—

*Antonio.* He could not miss't.

*Adrian.* It must needs be of subtle, tender, and delicate temperance.

*Antonio.* Temperance was a delicate wench.

*Sebastian.* Ay, and a subtle; as he most learnedly deliver'd.

*Adrian.* The air breathes upon us here most sweetly.

*Sebastian.* As if it had lungs, and rotten ones.

*Antonio.* Or as 'twere perfum'd by a fen.

*Gonzalo.* Here is every thing advantageous to life.

*Antonio.* True; save means to live.

*Sebastian.* Of that there's none, or little.

*Gonzalo.* How lush and lusty the grass looks! how green!

*Antonio.* The ground, indeed, is tawny.

*Sebastian.* With an eye of green in't.

*Antonio.* He misses not much.

*Sebastian.* No; he doth but mistake the truth totally.

*Gonzalo.* But the rarity of it is,—which is indeed almost beyond credit,—

*Sebastian.* As many vouch'd rarities are.

*Gonzalo.* That our garments, being, as they were, drench'd in the sea, hold, notwithstanding, their freshness and glosses, being rather new-dyed than stain'd with salt water.

*Antonio.* If but one of his pockets could speak, would it not say he lies?

*Sebastian.* Ay, or very falsely pocket up his report.

*Gonzalo.* Methinks our garments are now as fresh as when we put them on first in Afric, at the marriage of the king's fair daughter Claribel to the King of Tunis.

*Sebastian.* 'Twas a sweet marriage, and we prosper well in our return.

*Adrian.* Tunis was never grac'd before with such a paragon to their queen.

*Gonzalo.* Not since widow Dido's time.

*Antonio.* Widow! a plague o' that! How came that widow in? Widow Dido!

*Sebastian.* What if he had said widower Æneas too? Good Lord, how you take it!

*Adrian.* Widow Dido, said you? you make me study of that: she was of Carthage, not of Tunis.

*Gonzalo.* This Tunis, sir, was Carthage.

*Adrian.* Carthage?

*Gonzalo.* I assure you, Carthage.

*Antonio.* His word is more than the miraculous harp.

*Sebastian.* He hath rais'd the wall, and houses too.

*Antonio.* What impossible matter will he make easy next?

*Sebastian.* I think he will carry this island home in his pocket, and give it his son for an apple.

*Antonio.* And, sowing the kernels of it in the sea, bring forth more islands.

*Gonzalo.* Ay?

*Antonio.* Why, in good time.

*Gonzalo.* Sir, we were talking that our garments seem now as fresh as when we were at Tunis at the marriage of your daughter, who is now queen.

*Antonio.* And the rarest that e'er came there.

*Sebastian.* Bate, I beseech you, widow Dido.

*Antonio.* O, widow Dido! ay, widow Dido.

*Gonzalo.* Is not, sir, my doublet as fresh as the first day I wore it? I mean, in a sort.

*Antonio.* That sort was well fish'd for.

*Gonzalo.* When I wore it at your daughter's marriage?

*Alonso.* You cram these words into mine ears against
The stomach of my sense. Would I had never
Married my daughter there! for, coming thence,
My son is lost; and, in my rate, she too,
Who is so far from Italy remov'd
I ne'er again shall see her. O thou mine heir

Of Naples and of Milan, what strange fish
Hath made his meal on thee?

*Francisco.* Sir, he may live:
I saw him beat the surges under him,
And ride upon their backs; he trod the water,
Whose enmity he flung aside, and breasted
The surge most swoln that met him; his bold head
'Bove the contentious waves he kept, and oar'd
Himself with his good arms in lusty stroke
To th' shore, that o'er his wave-worn basis bow'd,
As stooping to relieve him. I not doubt,
He came alive to land.

*Alonso.* No, no, he's gone.

*Sebastian.* Sir, you may thank yourself for this great loss,
That would not bless our Europe with your daughter,
But rather lose her to an African;
Where she, at least, is banish'd from your eye,
Who hath cause to wet the grief on't.

*Alonso.* Prithee, peace.

*Sebastian.* You were kneel'd to, and importun'd otherwise,
By all of us; and the fair soul herself
Weigh'd, between loathness and obedience, at
Which end o' th' beam she'd bow. We have lost your son,
I fear, forever: Milan and Naples have
More widows in them of this business' making,
Than we bring men to comfort them: the fault's
Your own.

*Alonso.* So is the dear'st o' th' loss.

*Gonzalo.* My lord Sebastian,
The truth you speak doth lack some gentleness,
And time to speak it in: you rub the sore,
When you should bring the plaster.

*Sebastian.* Very well.

*Antonio.* And most chirurgeonly.

*Gonzalo.* It is foul weather in us all, good sir,
When you are cloudy.

*Sebastian.* Foul weather?

*Antonio.* Very foul.

*Gonzalo.* Had I plantation of this isle, my lord,—

*Antonio.* He'd sow't with nettle-seed.

*Sebastian.* Or docks, or mallows.

*Gonzalo.* And were the king on't, what would I do?

*Sebastian.* Scape being drunk, for want of wine.

*Gonzalo.* I' th' commonwealth I would by contraries
Execute all things; for no kind of traffic
Would I admit; no name of magistrate;
Letters should not be known; riches, poverty,
And use of service, none; contract, succession,
Bourn, bound of land, tilth, vineyard, none;
No use of metal, corn, or wine, or oil;
No occupation; all men idle, all;
And women too, but innocent and pure;
No sovereignty;—

*Sebastian.* Yet he would be king on't.

*Antonio.* The latter end of his commonwealth forgets the beginning.

*Gonzalo.* All things in common nature should produce
Without sweat or endeavour: treason, felony,
Sword, pike, knife, gun, or need of any engine,
Would I not have; but nature should bring forth,
Of it own kind, all foison, all abundance,
To feed my innocent people.

*Sebastian.* No marrying 'mong his subjects?

*Antonio.* None, man; all idle; whores and knaves.

*Gonzalo.* I would with such perfection góvern, sir,
T' excel the golden age.

*Sebastian.* Save his majesty!

*Antonio.* Long live Gonzalo!

*Gonzalo.* And,—do you mark me, sir?—

*Alonso.* Prithee, no more: thou dost talk nothing to me.

*Gonzalo.* I do well believe your highness; and did it to

minister occasion to these gentlemen, who are of such sensible and nimble lungs that they always use to laugh at nothing.

*Antonio.* 'Twas you we laugh'd at.

*Gonzalo.* Who, in this kind of merry fooling, am nothing to you: so you may continue, and laugh at nothing still.

*Antonio.* What a blow was there given!

*Sebastian.* An it had not fallen flat-long.

*Gonzalo.* You are gentlemen of brave mettle: you would lift the moon out of her sphere, if she would continue in it five weeks without changing.

*Enter* ARIEL (*invisible*) *playing solemn music.*

*Sebastian.* We would so, and then go a bat-fowling.

*Antonio.* Nay, good my lord, be not angry.

*Gonzalo.* No, I warrant you; I will not adventure my discretion so weakly. Will you laugh me asleep, for I am very heavy?

*Antonio.* Go sleep, and hear us.

[*All sleep except Alonso, Sebastian, and Antonio.*

*Alonso.* What, all so soon asleep! I wish mine eyes
Would, with themselves, shut up my thoughts: I find
They are inclin'd to do so.

*Sebastian.* Please you, sir,
Do not omit the heavy offer of it:
It seldom visits sorrow; when it doth,
It is a comforter.

*Antonio.* We two, my lord,
Will guard your person while you take your rest,
And watch your safety.

*Alonso.* Thank you.—Wondrous heavy.

[*Alonso sleeps. Exit Ariel.*

*Sebastian.* What a strange drowsiness possesses them!

*Antonio.* It is the quality o' th' climate.

*Sebastian.* Why

Doth it not then our eyelids sink? I find not
Myself dispos'd to sleep.

*Antonio.* Nor I; my spirits are nimble.
They fell together all, as by consent;
They dropp'd, as by a thunder-stroke. What might,
Worthy Sebastian?—O, what might?—No more:—
And yet methinks I see it in thy face,
What thou shouldst be: th' occasion speaks thee, and
My strong imagination sees a crown
Dropping upon thy head.

*Sebastian.* What, art thou waking?

*Antonio.* Do you not hear me speak?

*Sebastian.* I do; and surely
It is a sleepy language, and thou speak'st
Out of thy sleep. What is it thou didst say?
This is a strange repose, to be asleep
With eyes wide open; standing, speaking, moving,
And yet so fast asleep.

*Antonio.* Noble Sebastian,
Thou let'st thy fortune sleep—die, rather; wink'st
Whiles thou art waking.

*Sebastian.* Thou dost snore distinctly;
There's meaning in thy snores.

*Antonio.* I am more serious than my custom: you
Must be so too, if heed me; which to do,
Trebles thee o'er.

*Sebastian.* Well, I am standing water.

*Antonio.* I'll teach you how to flow.

*Sebastian.* Do so: to ebb
Hereditary sloth instructs me.

*Antonio.* O,
If you but knew how you the purpose cherish
Whiles thus you mock it! how, in stripping it,
You more invest it! Ebbing men indeed
Most often do so near the bottom run
By their own fear or sloth.

*Sebastian.* Prithee, say on:
The setting of thine eye and cheek proclaim
A matter from thee, and a birth, indeed,
Which throes thee much to yield.
*Antonio.* Thus, sir:
Although this lord of weak remembrance,—this,
Who shall be of as little memory
When he is earth'd,—hath here almost persuaded,—
For he's a spirit of persuasion, only
Professes to persuade,—the king his son's alive,
'Tis as impossible that he's undrown'd,
As he that sleeps here swims.
*Sebastian.* I have no hope
That he's undrown'd.
*Antonio.* O, out of that no hope
What great hope have you! no hope that way is
Another way so high a hope, that even
Ambition can not pierce a wink beyond,
But doubts discovery there. Will you grant with me
That Ferdinand is drown'd?
*Sebastian.* He's gone.
*Antonio.* Then, tell me,
Who's the next heir of Naples?
*Sebastian.* Claribel.
*Antonio.* She that is Queen of Tunis; she that dwells
Ten leagues beyond man's life; she that from Naples
Can have no note, unless the sun were post,—
The man i' th' moon's too slow,—till new-born chins
Be rough and razorable; she from whom
We all were sea-swallow'd, though some cast again;
And by that destiny to perform an act
Whereof what's past is prologue; what to come,
In yours and my discharge.
*Sebastian.* What stuff is this! How say you?
'Tis true, my brother's daughter's Queen of Tunis;

So is she heir of Naples ; 'twixt which regions
There is some space.
*Antonio.* A space whose every cubit
Seems to cry out, " How shall that Claribel
Measure us back to Naples ? Keep in Tunis,
And let Sebastian wake." Say, this were death
That now hath seiz'd them ; why, they were no worse
Than now they are. There be that can rule Naples
As well as he that sleeps ; lords that can prate
As amply and unnecessarily
As this Gonzalo : I myself could make
A chough of as deep chat. O, that you bore
The mind that I do ! what a sleep were this
For your advancement ! Do you understand me ?
*Sebastian.* Methinks I do.
*Antonio.* And how does your content
Tender your own good fortune ?
*Sebastian.* I remember
You did supplant your brother Prospero.
*Antonio.* True :
And look how well my garments sit upon me ;
Much feater than before. My brother's servants
Were then my fellows, now they are my men.
*Sebastian.* But, for your conscience—
*Antonio.* Ay, sir ; where lies that ? If 'twere a kibe,
'Twould put me to my slipper ; but I feel not
This deity in my bosom. Twenty consciences,
That stand 'twixt me and Milan, candied be they,
And melt, ere they molest ! Here lies your brother,
No better than the earth he lies upon,
If he were that which now he's like,—that's dead ;
Whom I, with this obedient steel, three inches of it,
Can lay to bed forever ; whiles you, doing thus,
To the perpetual wink for aye might put
This ancient morsel, this Sir Prudence, who

Should not upbraid our course. For all the rest,
They'll take suggestion as a cat laps milk;
They'll tell the clock to any business that
We say befits the hour.

*Sebastian.* Thy case, dear friend,
Shall be my precedent; as thou got'st Milan,
I'll come by Naples. Draw thy sword: one stroke
Shall free thee from the tribute which thou pay'st;
And I the king shall love thee.

*Antonio.* Draw together;
And when I rear my hand, do you the like,
To fall it on Gonzalo.

*Sebastian.* O, but one word. [*They talk apart.*

*Enter* ARIEL, *with music and song.*

*Ariel.* My master through his art foresees the danger
That you, his friend, are in; and sends me forth,—
For else his project dies,—to keep thee living.
[*Sings in Gonzalo's ear.*

*While you here do snoring lie,*
*Open-eyed conspiracy*
*His time doth take.*
*If of life you keep a care,*
*Shake off slumber, and beware:*
*Awake! Awake!*

*Antonio.* Then let us both be sudden.

*Gonzalo.* Now, good angels preserve the king!
[*They wake.*

*Alonso.* Why, how now? ho, awake!—Why are you drawn?
Wherefore this ghastly looking?

*Gonzalo.* What's the matter?

*Sebastian.* Whiles we stood here securing your repose,
Even now, we heard a hollow burst of bellowing
Like bulls, or rather lions: did't not wake you?
It struck mine ear most terribly.

*Alonso.* I heard nothing.

*Antonio.* O, 'twas a din to fright a monster's ear,
To make an earthquake: sure, it was the roar
Of a whole herd of lions.

*Alonso.* Heard you this, Gonzalo?

*Gonzalo.* Upon mine honour, sir, I heard a humming,—
And that a strange one too,—which did awake me:
I shak'd you, sir, and cried: as mine eyes open'd,
I saw their weapons drawn:—there was a noise,
That's verily. 'Tis best we stand upon our guard,
Or that we quit this place: let's draw our weapons.

*Alonso.* Lead off this ground; and let's make further search
For my poor son.

*Gonzalo.* Heavens keep him from these beasts!
For he is, sure, i' th' island.

*Alonso.* Lead away.

*Ariel.* Prospero my lord shall know what I have done:
So, king, go safely on to seek thy son. [*Exeunt.*

## SCENE II. *Another part of the island.*

*Enter* CALIBAN, *with a burthen of wood. A noise of thunder heard.*

*Caliban.* All the infections that the sun sucks up
From bogs, fens, flats, on Prosper fall, and make him
By inch-meal a disease! His spirits hear me,
And yet I needs must curse. But they'll nor pinch,
Fright me with urchin-shows, pitch me i' th' mire,
Nor lead me, like a fire-brand, in the dark
Out of my way, unless he bid 'em: but
For every trifle are they set upon me;
Sometime like apes, that mow and chatter at me,
And after bite me; then like hedgehogs, which
Lie tumbling in my barefoot way, and mount
Their pricks at my footfall; sometime am I

All wound with adders, who with cloven tongues
Do hiss me into madness.—

*Enter* TRINCULO.

Lo, now, lo!
Here comes a spirit of his, and to torment me
For bringing wood in slowly. I'll fall flat;
Perchance he will not mind me.

*Trinculo.* Here's neither bush nor shrub, to bear off any weather at all, and another storm brewing: I hear it sing i' th' wind. Yond same black cloud, yond huge one, looks like a foul bombard that would shed his liquor. If it should thunder as it did before, I know not where to hide my head: yond same cloud cannot choose but fall by pailfuls.—What have we here? a man or a fish? dead or alive? A fish: he smells like a fish; a very ancient and fish-like smell; a kind of, not of the newest, Poor-John. A strange fish! Were I in England now, as once I was, and had but this fish painted, not a holiday fool there but would give a piece of silver: there would this monster make a man: any strange beast there makes a man. When they will not give a doit to relieve a lame beggar, they will lay out ten to see a dead Indian. Legg'd like a man! and his fins like arms! Warm o' my troth! I do now let loose my opinion, hold it no longer: this is no fish, but an islander, that hath lately suffered by a thunderbolt. [*Thunder.*] Alas, the storm is come again! my best way is to creep under his gaberdine; there is no other shelter hereabout. Misery acquaints a man with strange bedfellows. I will here shroud till the dregs of the storm be past.

*Enter* STEPHANO, *singing: a bottle in his hand.*

Stephano. *I shall no more to sea, to sea,*
*Here shall I die ashore,—*

This is a very scurvy tune to sing at a man's funeral. Well, here's my comfort. [*Drinks.*

[Sings.] *The master, the swabber, the boatswain, and I,*
*The gunner, and his mate,*
*Loved Mall, Meg, and Marian, and Margery,*
*But none of us car'd for Kate;*
*For she had a tongue with a tang,*
*Would cry to a sailor, Go hang!*
*Then, to sea, boys, and let her go hang!*

This is a scurvy tune too; but here's my comfort. [*Drinks.*

*Caliban.* Do not torment me:—O!

*Stephano.* What's the matter? Have we devils here? Do you put tricks upon's with savages and men of Ind, ha? I have not scap'd drowning to be afeard now of your four legs; for it hath been said, as proper a man as ever went on four legs cannot make him give ground; and it shall be said so again, while Stephano breathes at nostrils.

*Caliban.* The spirit torments me:—O!

*Stephano.* This is some monster of the isle with four legs, who hath got, as I take it, an ague. Where the devil should he learn our language? I will give him some relief, if it be but for that. If I can recover him, and keep him tame, and get to Naples with him, he's a present for any emperor that ever trod on neat's-leather.

*Caliban.* Do not torment me, prithee; I'll bring my wood home faster.

*Stephano.* He's in his fit now, and does not talk after the wisest. He shall taste of my bottle: if he have never drunk wine afore, it will go near to remove his fit. If I can recover him, and keep him tame, I will not take too much for him; he shall pay for him that hath him, and that soundly.

*Caliban.* Thou dost me yet but little hurt; thou wilt anon, I know it by thy trembling: now Prosper works upon thee.

*Stephano.* Come on your ways; open your mouth; here is that which will give language to you, cat. Open your mouth; this will shake your shaking, I can tell you, and that soundly: you cannot tell who's your friend: open your chaps again.

*Trinculo.* I should know that voice: it should be—but he is drown'd; and these are devils:—O, defend me!

*Stephano.* Four legs and two voices! a most delicate monster! His forward voice, now, is to speak well of his friend; his backward voice is to utter foul speeches and to detract. If all the wine in my bottle will recover him, I will help his ague. Come:—Amen! I will pour some in thy other mouth.

*Trinculo.* Stephano!

*Stephano.* Doth thy other mouth call me? Mercy, mercy! This is a devil, and no monster: I will leave him; I have no long spoon.

*Trinculo.* Stephano! If thou beest Stephano, touch me, and speak to me; for I am Trinculo,—be not afeard,—thy good friend Trinculo.

*Stephano.* If thou beest Trinculo, come forth: I'll pull thee by the lesser legs: if any be Trinculo's legs, these are they. Thou art very Trinculo indeed! How camest thou to be the siege of this moon-calf? Can he vent Trinculos?

*Trinculo.* I took him to be kill'd with a thunder-stroke.—But art thou not drown'd, Stephano? I hope, now, thou art not drown'd. Is the storm overblown? I hid me under the dead moon-calf's gaberdine for fear of the storm. And art thou living, Stephano? O Stephano, two Neapolitans scap'd?

*Stephano.* Prithee, do not turn me about; my stomach is not constant.

*Caliban.* These be fine things, an if they be not sprites.
That's a brave god, and bears celestial liquor:
I will kneel to him.

*Stephano.* How didst thou scape? How camest thou hither? swear, by this bottle, how thou camest hither. I escap'd upon a butt of sack, which the sailors heaved o'erboard, by this bottle!—which I made of the bark of a tree with mine own hands, since I was cast ashore.

*Caliban.* I'll swear, upon that bottle, to be thy true subject;
For the liquor is not earthly.

*Stephano.* Here; swear, then, how thou escapedst.

*Trinculo.* Swam ashore, man, like a duck: I can swim like a duck, I'll be sworn.

*Stephano.* Here, kiss the book. Though thou canst swim like a duck, thou art made like a goose.

*Trinculo.* O Stephano, hast any more of this?

*Stephano.* The whole butt, man: my cellar is in a rock by th' sea-side, where my wine is hid. How now, moon-calf! how does thine ague?

*Caliban.* Hast thou not dropp'd from heaven?

*Stephano.* Out o' th' moon, I do assure thee: I was the man i' th' moon when time was.

*Caliban.* I have seen thee in her, and I do adore thee:
My mistress show'd me thee, and thy dog, and thy bush.

*Stephano.* Come, swear to that; kiss the book: I will furnish it anon with new contents: swear.

*Trinculo.* By this good light, this is a very shallow monster! —I afeard of him!—A very weak monster!—The man i' th' moon!—A most poor credulous monster!—Well drawn, monster, in good sooth!

*Caliban.* I'll show thee every fertile inch o' th' island;
And I will kiss thy foot. I prithee, be my god.

*Trinculo.* By this light, a most perfidious and drunken monster! When's god's asleep, he'll rob his bottle.

*Caliban.* I'll kiss thy foot; I'll swear myself thy subject.

*Stephano.* Come on, then; down, and swear.

*Trinculo.* I shall laugh myself to death at this puppy-headed monster. A most scurvy monster! I could find in my heart to beat him,—

*Stephano.* Come, kiss.

*Trinculo.* But that the poor monster's in drink. An abominable monster!

*Caliban.* I'll show thee the best springs; I'll pluck thee [berries;

I'll fish for thee, and get thee wood enough.
A plague upon the tyrant that I serve!
I'll bear him no more sticks, but follow thee,
Thou wondrous man.

*Trinculo.* A most ridiculous monster, to make a wonder of a poor drunkard!

*Caliban.* I prithee, let me bring thee where crabs grow;
And I with my long nails will dig thee pig-nuts,
Show thee a jay's nest, and instruct thee how
To snare the nimble marmoset. I'll bring thee
To clustering filberts; and sometimes I'll get thee
Young scamels from the rock. Wilt thou go with me?

*Stephano.* I prithee now, lead the way without any more talking.—Trinculo, the king and all our company else being drown'd, we will inherit here.—Here, bear my bottle.—Fellow Trinculo, we'll fill him by and by again.

*Caliban* [*sings drunkenly*]. Farewell, master; farewell, farewell!

*Trinculo.* A howling monster; a drunken monster!

Caliban. *No more dams I'll make for fish;*
*Nor fetch in firing*
*At requiring;*
*Nor scrape trenchering, nor wash dish:*
*'Ban, 'Ban, Ca-caliban*
*Has a new master:—get a new man.*

Freedom, hey-day! hey-day, freedom! freedom, hey-day, freedom!

*Stephano.* O brave monster! Lead the way. [*Exeunt.*

## ACT III.

SCENE I. *Before* PROSPERO'S *cell.*

*Enter* FERDINAND, *bearing a log.*

*Ferdinand.* There be some sports are painful, and their la-
Delight in them sets off: some kinds of baseness [bour
Are nobly undergone, and most poor matters

Point to rich ends. This my mean task
Would be as heavy to me as odious, but
The mistress which I serve quickens what's dead,
And makes my labours pleasures. O, she is
Ten times more gentle than her father's crabbed,
And he's compos'd of harshness! I must remove
Some thousands of these logs, and pile them up,
Upon a sore injunction. My sweet mistress
Weeps when she sees me work, and says, such baseness
Had never like executor. I forget:
But these sweet thoughts do even refresh my labours,
Most busy, least when I do it.

*Enter* MIRANDA, *and* PROSPERO *at a distance.*

*Miranda.* Alas! now, pray you,
Work not so hard: I would the lightning had
Burnt up those logs that you are enjoin'd to pile!
Pray, set it down, and rest you; when this burns,
'Twill weep for having wearied you. My father
Is hard at study; pray, now, rest yourself;
He's safe for these three hours.

*Ferdinand.* O most dear mistress,
The sun will set before I shall discharge
What I must strive to do.

*Miranda.* If you'll sit down,
I'll bear your logs the while. Pray, give me that;
I'll carry it to the pile.

*Ferdinand.* No, precious creature;
I'd rather crack my sinews, break my back,
Than you should such dishonour undergo,
While I sit lazy by.

*Miranda.* It would become me
As well as it does you; and I should do it
With much more ease, for my good will is to it,
And yours it is against.

*Prospero.* Poor worm, thou art infected!
This visitation shows it.
*Miranda.* You look wearily.
*Ferdinand.* No, noble mistress; 'tis fresh morning with me
When you are by at night. I do beseech you,—
Chiefly that I might set it in my prayers,—
What is your name?
*Miranda.* Miranda.—O my father,
I have broken your hest to say so!
*Ferdinand.* Admir'd Miranda!
Indeed the top of admiration; worth
What's dearest to the world! Full many a lady
I have eyed with best regard, and many a time
Th' harmony of their tongues hath into bondage
Brought my too diligent ear. For several virtues
Have I lik'd several women; never any
With so full soul, but some defect in her
Did quarrel with the noblest grace she owed,
And put it to the foil: but you, O you,
So perfect and so peerless, are created
Of every creature's best!
*Miranda.* I do not know
One of my sex; no woman's face remember,
Save, from my glass, mine own; nor have I seen
More that I may call men than you, good friend,
And my dear father. How features are abroad,
I am skilless of; but, by my modesty,
The jewel in my dower, I would not wish
Any companion in the world but you;
Nor can imagination form a shape,
Besides yourself, to like of.—But I prattle
Something too wildly, and my father's precepts
I therein do forget.
*Ferdinand.* I am, in my condition,
A prince, Miranda; I do think, a king;—

I would, not so!—and would no more endure
This wooden slavery than to suffer
The flesh-fly blow my mouth. Hear my soul speak:
The very instant that I saw you, did
My heart fly to your service; there resides,
To make me slave to it; and for your sake
Am I this patient log-man.

*Miranda.* Do you love me?

*Ferdinand.* O heaven! O earth! bear witness to this [sound.
And crown what I profess with kind event,
If I speak true; if hollowly, invert
What best is boded me to mischief! I,
Beyond all limit of what else i' th' world,
Do love, prize, honour you.

*Miranda.* I am a fool
To weep at what I am glad of.

*Prospero.* Fair encounter
Of two most rare affections! Heavens rain grace
On that which breeds between 'em!

*Ferdinand.* Wherefore weep you?

*Miranda.* At mine unworthiness, that dare not offer
What I desire to give; and, much less, take
What I shall die to want. But this is trifling;
And all the more it seeks to hide itself,
The bigger bulk it shows. Hence, bashful cunning!
And prompt me, plain and holy innocence!
I am your wife, if you will marry me;
If not, I'll die your maid: to be your fellow
You may deny me; but I'll be your servant,
Whether you will or no.

*Ferdinand.* My mistress, dearest;
And I thus humble ever.

*Miranda.* My husband, then?

*Ferdinand.* Ay, with a heart as willing
As bondage e'er of freedom: here's my hand.

*Miranda.* And mine, with my heart in't: and now farewell
Till half an hour hence.

*Ferdinand.* A thousand thousand!

[*Exeunt Ferdinand and Miranda.*

*Prospero.* So glad of this as they I cannot be,
Who are surpris'd with all; but my rejoicing
At nothing can be more. I'll to my book;
For yet ere supper-time must I perform
Much business appertaining. [*Exit.*

SCENE II. *Another part of the island.*

*Enter* CALIBAN, STEPHANO, *and* TRINCULO.

*Stephano.* Tell not me:—when the butt is out, we will drink water; not a drop before: therefore bear up, and board 'em. Servant-monster, drink to me.

*Trinculo.* Servant-monster! the folly of this island! They say there's but five upon this isle: we are three of them; if th' other two be brain'd like us, the State totters.

*Stephano.* Drink, servant-monster, when I bid thee: thy eyes are almost set in thy head.

*Trinculo.* Where should they be set else? he were a brave monster indeed, if they were set in his tail.

*Stephano.* My man-monster hath drown'd his tongue in sack: for my part, the sea cannot drown me; I swam, ere I could recover the shore, five-and-thirty leagues off and on, by this light! Thou shalt be my lieutenant, monster, or my standard.

*Trinculo.* Your lieutenant, if you list; he's no standard.

*Stephano.* We'll not run, Monsieur Monster.

*Trinculo.* Nor go neither; but you'll lie, like dogs, and yet say nothing neither.

*Stephano.* Moon-calf, speak once in thy life, if thou beest a good moon-calf.

*Caliban.* How does thy honour? Let me lick thy shoe. I'll not serve him, he is not valiant.

*Trinculo.* Thou liest, most ignorant monster: I am in case to justle a constable. Why, thou debosh'd fish, thou, was there ever man a coward, that hath drunk so much sack as I to-day? Wilt thou tell a monstrous lie, being but half a fish and half a monster?

*Caliban.* Lo, how he mocks me! wilt thou let him, my lord?

*Trinculo.* Lord, quoth he!—That a monster should be such a natural!

*Caliban.* Lo, lo, again! bite him to death, I prithee.

*Stephano.* Trinculo, keep a good tongue in your head: if you prove a mutineer,—the next tree! The poor monster's my subject, and he shall not suffer indignity.

*Caliban.* I thank my noble lord. Wilt thou be pleased
To hearken once again to the suit I made to thee?

*Stephano.* Marry, will I: kneel and repeat it; I will stand, and so shall Trinculo.

*Enter* ARIEL, *invisible.*

*Caliban.* As I told thee before, I am subject to a tyrant,
A sorcerer, that by his cunning hath cheated me
Of the island.

*Ariel.* Thou liest.

*Caliban.* Thou liest, thou jesting monkey, thou:
I would my valiant master would destroy thee!
I do not lie.

*Stephano.* Trinculo, if you trouble him any more in's tale, by this hand, I will supplant some of your teeth.

*Trinculo.* Why, I said nothing.

*Stephano.* Mum, then, and no more.—Proceed.

*Caliban.* I say, by sorcery he got this isle;
From me he got it. If thy greatness will,
Revenge it on him, for I know thou dar'st,
But this thing dare not.

*Stephano.* That's most certain.

*Caliban.* Thou shalt be lord of it, and I'll serve thee.

*Stephano.* How now shall this be compass'd? Canst thou bring me to the party?

*Caliban.* Yea, yea, my lord: I'll yield him thee asleep,
Where thou mayst knock a nail into his head.

*Ariel.* Thou liest; thou canst not.

*Caliban.* What a pied ninny's this! Thou scurvy patch!—
I do beseech thy greatness, give him blows,
And take his bottle from him: when that's gone,
He shall drink nought but brine; for I'll not show him
Where the quick freshes are.

*Stephano.* Trinculo, run into no further danger: interrupt the monster one word further, and, by this hand, I'll turn my mercy out o' doors, and make a stock-fish of thee.

*Trinculo.* Why, what did I? I did nothing. I'll go farther off.

*Stephano.* Didst thou not say he lied?

*Ariel.* Thou liest.

*Stephano.* Do I so? take thou that. [*Beats him.*] As you like this, give me the lie another time.

*Trinculo.* I did not give the lie. Out o' your wits, and hearing too?—A pox o' your bottle! this can sack and drinking do.—A murrain on your monster, and the devil take your fingers!

*Caliban.* Ha, ha, ha!

*Stephano.* Now, forward with your tale.—Prithee, stand further off.

*Caliban.* Beat him enough: after a little time,
I'll beat him too.

*Stephano.* Stand farther.—Come, proceed.

*Caliban.* Why, as I told thee, 'tis a custom with him
I' th' afternoon to sleep: there thou mayst brain him,
Having first seiz'd his books; or with a log
Batter his skull, or paunch him with a stake,
Or cut his wezand with thy knife. Remember
First to possess his books; for without them

He's but a sot, as I am, nor hath not
One spirit to command: they all do hate him
As rootedly as I. Burn but his books.
He has brave utensils,—for so he calls them,—
Which, when he has a house, he'll deck withal.
And that most deeply to consider is
The beauty of his daughter. He himself
Calls her a nonpareil: I never saw a woman,
But only Sycorax my dam and she;
But she as far surpasseth Sycorax
As great'st does least.

*Stephano.* Is it so brave a lass?

*Caliban.* Ay, lord: she will become thy bed, I warrant,
And bring thee forth brave brood.

*Stephano.* Monster, I will kill this man: his daughter and I will be king and queen,—save our graces!—and Trinculo and thyself shall be viceroys. Dost thou like the plot, Trinculo?

*Trinculo.* Excellent.

*Stephano.* Give me thy hand: I am sorry I beat thee; but, while thou liv'st, keep a good tongue in thy head.

*Caliban.* Within this half hour will he be asleep:
Wilt thou destroy him then?

*Stephano.* Ay, on mine honour.

*Ariel.* This will I tell my master.

*Caliban.* Thou mak'st me merry; I am full of pleasure.
Let us be jocund: will you troll the catch
You taught me but while-ere?

*Stephano.* At thy request, monster, I will do reason, any reason.—Come on, Trinculo, let us sing. [*Sings.*

*Flout 'em and scout 'em, and scout 'em and flout em;*
*Thought is free.*

*Caliban.* That's not the tune.

[*Ariel plays the tune on a tabor and pipe.*

*Stephano.* What is this same?

*Trinculo.* This is the tune of our catch, played by the picture of Nobody.

*Stephano.* If thou beest a man, show thyself in thy likeness: if thou beest a devil, take't as thou list.

*Trinculo.* O, forgive me my sins!

*Stephano.* He that dies pays all debts: I defy thee.—Mercy upon us!

*Caliban.* Art thou afeard?

*Stephano.* No, monster, not I.

*Caliban.* Be not afeard; the isle is full of noises,
Sounds and sweet airs, that give delight and hurt not.
Sometimes a thousand twangling instruments
Will hum about mine ears; and sometimes voices,
That, if I then had wak'd after long sleep,
Will make me sleep again: and then, in dreaming,
The clouds methought would open, and show riches
Ready to drop upon me; that, when I wak'd,
I cried to dream again.

*Stephano.* This will prove a brave kingdom to me, where I shall have my music for nothing.

*Caliban.* When Prospero is destroy'd.

*Stephano.* That shall be by and by: I remember the story.

*Trinculo.* The sound is going away; let's follow it, and after do our work.

*Stephano.* Lead, monster; we'll follow.—I would I could see this taborer; he lays it on.

*Trinculo.* Wilt come? I'll follow, Stephano. [*Exeunt.*

SCENE III. *Another part of the island.*

*Enter* ALONSO, SEBASTIAN, ANTONIO, GONZALO, ADRIAN, FRANCISCO, *and others.*

*Gonzalo.* By'r lakin, I can go no further, sir;
My old bones aches: here's a maze trod, indeed,

Through forth-rights and meanders! By your patience,
I needs must rest me.

*Alonso.* Old lord, I cannot blame thee,
Who am myself attach'd with weariness,
To th' dulling of my spirits: sit down, and rest.
Even here I will put off my hope, and keep it
No longer for my flatterer: he is drown'd
Whom thus we stray to find; and the sea mocks
Our frustrate search on land. Well, let him go.

*Antonio* [*Aside to Sebastian*]. I am right glad that he's so out of hope.
Do not, for one repulse, forego the purpose
That you resolv'd t' effect.

*Sebastian* [*Aside to Antonio*]. The next advantage
Will we take throughly.

*Antonio* [*Aside to Sebastian*]. Let it be to-night;
For, now they are oppress'd with travel, they
Will not, nor cannot, use such vigilance
As when they are fresh.

*Sebastian* [*Aside to Antonio*]. I say, to-night: no more.
[*Solemn and strange music.*

*Alonso.* What harmony is this?—My good friends, hark!

*Gonzalo.* Marvellous sweet music!

*Enter* PROSPERO *above, invisible. Enter several strange Shapes, bringing in a banquet: they dance about it with gentle actions of salutation; and, inviting the King, etc. to eat, they depart.*

*Alonso.* Give us kind keepers, heavens!—What were these?

*Sebastian.* A living drollery. Now I will believe
That there are unicorns; that in Arabia
There is one tree, the phœnix' throne; one phœnix
At this hour reigning there.

*Antonio.* I'll believe both;
And what does else want credit, come to me,
And I'll be sworn 'tis true: travelers ne'er did lie,
Though fools at home condemn 'em.

*Gonzalo.* If in Naples
I should report this now, would they believe me?
If I should say, I saw such islanders,—
For, certes, these are people of the island,—
Who, though they are of monstrous shape, yet, note,
Their manners are more gentle, kind, than of
Our human generation you shall find
Many, nay, almost any.

*Prospero* [*Aside*]. Honest lord,
Thou hast said well; for some of you there present
Are worse than devils.

*Alonso.* I cannot too much muse
Such shapes, such gesture, and such sound, expressing—
Although they want the use of tongue—a kind
Of excellent dumb discourse.

*Prospero* [*Aside*]. Praise in departing.

*Francisco.* They vanish'd strangely.

*Sebastian.* No matter, since
They have left their viands behind; for we have stomachs.—
Will't please you taste of what is here?

*Alonso.* Not I.

*Gonzalo.* Faith, sir, you need not fear. When we were boys,
Who would believe that there were mountaineers
Dew-lapp'd like bulls, whose throats had hanging at 'em
Wallets of flesh? or that there were such men
Whose heads stood in their breasts? which now we find
Each putter-out of five for one will bring us
Good warrant of.

*Alonso.* I will stand to, and feed,
Although my last: no matter, since I feel
The best is past.—Brother, my lord the duke,
Stand to, and do as we.

*Thunder and lightning. Enter* ARIEL, *like a harpy, claps his wings upon the table, and with a quaint device the banquet vanishes.*

*Ariel.* You are three men of sin, whom destiny,—
That hath to instrument this lower world
And what is in't,—the never-surfeited sea
Hath caus'd to belch up you; and on this island,
Where man doth not inhabit,—you 'mongst men
Being most unfit to live. I have made you mad;
And even with such-like valour men hang and drown
Their proper selves. [*Alonso, Sebastian, etc., draw their swords.*
You fools! I and my fellows
Are ministers of Fate: the elements,
Of whom your swords are temper'd, may as well
Wound the loud winds, or with bemock'd-at stabs
Kill the still-closing waters, as diminish
One dowle that's in my plume. My fellow-ministers
Are like invulnerable. If you could hurt,
Your swords are now too massy for your strengths,
And will not be uplifted. But remember,—
For that's my business to you,—that you three
From Milan did supplant good Prospero;
Expos'd unto the sea, which hath requit it,
Him and his innocent child: for which foul deed
The powers, delaying, not forgetting, have
Incens'd the seas and shores, yea, all the creatures
Against your peace. Thee of thy son, Alonso,
They have bereft; and do pronounce by me,
Lingering perdition—worse than any death
Can be at once—shall step by step attend
You and your ways; whose wraths to guard you from,—
Which here, in this most desolate isle, else falls
Upon your heads,—is nothing but heart's sorrow,
And a clear life ensuing.

*He vanishes in thunder; then, to soft music, enter the Shapes again, and dance with mocks and mows, and carry out the table.*

*Prospero* [*Aside*]. Bravely the figure of this harpy hast thou
Perform'd, my Ariel; a grace it had, devouring.
Of my instruction hast thou nothing bated
In what thou hadst to say: so, with good life
And observation strange, my meaner ministers
Their several kinds have done. My high charms work,
And these mine enemies are all knit up
In their distractions: they now are in my power;
And in these fits I leave them, while I visit
Young Ferdinand,—whom they suppose is drown'd,—
And his and mine lov'd darling. [*Exit above.*

*Gonzalo.* I' th' name of something holy, sir, why stand you
In this strange stare?

*Alonso.* O, it is monstrous, monstrous!
Methought the billows spoke, and told me of it;
The winds did sing it to me; and the thunder,
That deep and dreadful organ-pipe, pronounc'd
The name of Prosper: it did bass my trespass.
Therefore my son i' th' ooze is bedded; and
I'll seek him deeper than e'er plummet sounded,
And with him there lie mudded. [*Exit.*

*Sebastian.* But one fiend at a time,
I'll fight their legions o'er.

*Antonio.* I'll be thy second.
[*Exeunt Sebastian and Antonio.*

*Gonzalo.* All three of them are desperate: their great guilt,
Like poison given to work a great time after,
Now 'gins to bite the spirits.—I do beseech you
That are of suppler joints, follow them swiftly,
And hinder them from what this ecstasy
May now provoke them to.

*Adrian.* Follow, I pray you. [*Exeunt.*

# ACT IV.

## SCENE I. *Before* PROSPERO'S *cell.*

*Enter* PROSPERO, FERDINAND, *and* MIRANDA.

*Prospero.* If I have too austerely punish'd you,
Your compensation makes amends; for I
Have given you here a thread of mine own life,

Or that for which I live: who once again
I tender to thy hand. All thy vexations
Were but my trials of thy love, and thou
Hast strangely stood the test: here, afore Heaven,
I ratify this my rich gift. O Ferdinand,
Do not smile at me that I boast her off,
For thou shalt find she will outstrip all praise,
And make it halt behind her.

*Ferdinand.* I do believe it
Against an oracle.

*Prospero.* Then, as my gift and thine own acquisition
Worthily purchas'd, take my daughter: but
If thou dost break her virgin-knot before
All sanctimonious ceremonies may
With full and holy rite be minister'd,
No sweet aspersion shall the heavens let fall
To make this contract grow; but barren hate,
Sour-eyed disdain, and discord shall bestrew
The union of your bed with weeds so loathly
That you shall hate it both: therefore, take heed,
As Hymen's lamps shall light you.

*Ferdinand.* As I hope
For quiet days, fair issue, and long life,
With such love as 'tis now, the murkiest den,
The most opportune place, the strong'st suggestion
Our worser genius can, shall never melt
Mine honour into lust, to take away
The edge of that day's celebration
When I shall think, or Phœbus' steeds are founder'd,
Or night kept chain'd below.

*Prospero.* Fairly spoke.
Sit then and talk with her; she is thine own.—
What, Ariel! my industrious servant, Ariel!

*Enter* ARIEL.

*Ariel.* What would my potent master? here I am.

*Prospero.* Thou and thy meaner fellows your last service
Did worthily perform; and I must use you
In such another trick. Go bring the rabble,
O'er whom I give thee power, here to this place:
Incite them to quick motion, for I must
Bestow upon the eyes of this young couple
Some vanity of mine art: it is my promise,
And they expect it from me.

*Ariel.* Presently?

*Prospero.* Ay, with a twink.

*Ariel.* Before you can say, 'come,' and 'go,'
And breathe twice, and cry, 'so, so,'
Each one, tripping on his toe,
Will be here with mop and mow.—
Do you love me, master? no?

*Prospero.* Dearly, my delicate Ariel. Do not approach
Till thou dost hear me call.

*Ariel.* Well, I conceive. [*Exit.*

*Prospero.* Look thou be true; do not give dalliance
Too much the rein: the strongest oaths are straw
To th' fire i' th' blood; be more abstemious,
Or else, good night your vow!

*Ferdinand.* I warrant you, sir;
The white-cold virgin snow upon my heart
Abates the ardour of my liver.

*Prospero.* Well.—
Now come, my Ariel! bring a corollary,
Rather than want a spirit: appear, and pertly!—
No tongue! all eyes! be silent. [*Soft music.*

*Enter* IRIS.

*Iris.* Ceres, most bounteous lady, thy rich leas

Of wheat, rye, barley, vetches, oats, and pease;
Thy turfy mountains, where live nibbling sheep,
And flat meads thatch'd with stover, them to keep;
Thy banks with pioned and lilied brims,
Which spongy April at thy hest betrims,
To make cold nymphs chaste crowns; and thy broom groves,
Whose shadow the dismissed bachelor loves,
Being lass-lorn; thy pole-clipt vineyard;
And thy sea-marge, sterile and rocky-hard,
Where thou thyself dost air;—the queen o' th' sky,
Whose watery arch and messenger am I,
Bids thee leave these; and with her sovereign grace,
Here on this grass-plot, in this very place,
To come and sport.—Her peacocks fly amain:
Approach, rich Ceres, her to entertain.

*Enter* CERES.

*Ceres.* Hail, many-colour'd messenger, that ne'er
Dost disobey the wife of Jupiter;
Who, with thy saffron wings, upon my flowers
Diffusest honey-drops, refreshing showers;
And with each end of thy blue bow dost crown
My bosky acres and my unshrubb'd down,
Rich scarf to my proud earth! Why hath thy queen
Summon'd me hither, to this short-grass'd green?
*Iris.* A contract of true love to celebrate;
And some donation freely to estate
On the blest lovers.
*Ceres.* Tell me, heavenly bow,
If Venus or her son, as thou dost know,
Do now attend the queen? Since they did plot
The means that dusky Dis my daughter got,
Her and her blind boy's scandal'd company
I have forsworn.
*Iris.* Of her society

Be not afraid : I met her deity
Cutting the clouds towards Paphos, and her son
Dove-drawn with her. Here thought they to have done
Some wanton charm upon this man and maid,
Whose vows are, that no bed-right shall be paid
Till Hymen's torch be lighted : but in vain ;
Mars's hot minion is return'd again ;
Her waspish-headed son has broke his arrows,
Swears he will shoot no more, but play with sparrows,
And be a boy right out.

*Ceres.* Highest queen of state,
Great Juno comes ; I know her by her gait.

*Enter* JUNO.

*Juno.* How does my bounteous sister? Go with me
To bless this twain, that they may prosperous be,
And honour'd in their issue. [*They sing:*

Juno. *Honour, riches, marriage, blessing,*
*Long continuance, and increasing,*
*Hourly joys be still upon you!*
*Juno sings her blessings on you.*

Ceres. *Earth's increase, foison plenty,*
*Barns and garners never empty;*
*Vines with clustering bunches growing;*
*Plants with goodly burthen bowing;*
*Spring come to you at the farthest*
*In the very end of harvest!*
*Scarcity and want shall shun you;*
*Ceres' blessing so is on you.*

*Ferdinand.* This is a most majestic vision, and
Harmonious charmingly. May I be bold
To think these spirits?

*Prospero.* Spirits, which by mine art
I have from their confines call'd to enact
My present fancies.

*Ferdinand.* Let me live here ever;
So rare a wonder'd father and a wise
Makes this place Paradise.

[*Juno and Ceres whisper, and send Iris on employment.*

*Prospero.* Sweet now, silence!
Juno and Ceres whisper seriously;
There's something else to do: hush, and be mute,
Or else our spell is marr'd.

*Iris.* You nymphs, call'd Naiads, of the winding brooks,
With your sedg'd crowns and ever harmless looks,
Leave your crisp channels, and on this green land
Answer your summons; Juno does command.
Come, temperate nymphs, and help to celebrate
A contract of true love; be not too late.

*Enter certain Nymphs.*

You sunburnt sicklemen, of August weary,
Come hither from the furrow, and be merry.
Make holiday; your rye-straw hats put on,
And these fresh nymphs encounter every one
In country footing.

*Enter certain Reapers, properly habited: they join with the Nymphs in a graceful dance, towards the end whereof* PROSPERO *starts suddenly, and speaks; after which, to a strange, hollow, and confused noise, they heavily vanish.*

*Prospero* [*Aside*]. I had forgot that foul conspiracy
Of the beast Caliban and his confederates
Against my life; the minute of their plot
Is almost come.—[*To the Spirits.*] Well done! Avoid; no more!

*Ferdinand.* This is strange: your father's in some passion
That works him strongly.

*Miranda.* Never till this day
Saw I him touch'd with anger so distemper'd.

*Prospero.* You do look, my son, in a mov'd sort,
As if you were dismay'd : be cheerful, sir.
Our revels now are ended. These our actors,
As I foretold you, were all spirits, and
Are melted into air, into thin air :
And, like the baseless fabric of this vision,
The cloud-capp'd towers, the gorgeous palaces,
The solemn temples, the great globe itself,
Yea, all which it inherit, shall dissolve,
And, like this insubstantial pageant faded,
Leave not a rack behind. We are such stuff
As dreams are made on ; and our little life
Is rounded with a sleep.—Sir, I am vex'd ;
Bear with my weakness ; my old brain is troubled :
Be not disturb'd with my infirmity :
If you be pleas'd, retire into my cell
And there repose : a turn or two I'll walk,
To still my beating mind.

*Ferdinand. Miranda.* We wish your peace. [*Exeunt.*

*Prospero.* Come with a thought. I thank thee, Ariel : come!

*Enter* ARIEL.

*Ariel.* Thy thoughts I cleave to. What's thy pleasure?

*Prospero.* Spirit,
We must prepare to meet with Caliban.

*Ariel.* Ay, my commander : when I presented Ceres,
I thought to have told thee of it ; but I fear'd
Lest I might anger thee.

*Prospero.* Say again, where didst thou leave these varlets?

*Ariel.* I told you, sir, they were red-hot with drinking ;
So full of valour that they smote the air
For breathing in their faces, beat the ground
For kissing of their feet, yet always bending
Towards their project. Then I beat my tabor ;
At which, like unback'd colts, they prick'd their ears,

Advanc'd their eyelids, lifted up their noses
As they smelt music : so I charm'd their ears,
That, calf-like, they my lowing follow'd through
Tooth'd briers, sharp furzes, pricking gorse, and thorns,
Which enter'd their frail shins : at last I left them
I' th' filthy mantled pool beyond your cell,
There dancing up to th' chins, that the foul lake
O'erstunk their feet.
*Prospero.* This was well done, my bird.
Thy shape invisible retain thou still :
The trumpery in my house, go bring it hither,
For stale to catch these thieves.
*Ariel.* I go, I go. [*Exit.*
*Prospero.* A devil, a born devil, on whose nature
Nurture can never stick ; on whom my pains,
Humanely taken, all, all lost, quite lost ;
And as with age his body uglier grows,
So his mind cankers. I will plague them all,
Even to roaring.—

*Enter* ARIEL, *loaden with glistering apparel, etc.*

Come hang them on this line.

PROSPERO *and* ARIEL *remain invisible.* *Enter* CALIBAN, STEPHANO, *and* TRINCULO, *all wet.*

*Caliban.* Pray you, tread softly, that the blind mole may not
Hear a foot fall : we now are near his cell.

*Stephano.* Monster, your fairy, which you say is a harmless fairy, has done little better than play'd the Jack with us.—Do you hear, monster? If I should take a displeasure against you, look you,—

*Trinculo.* Thou wert but a lost monster.

*Caliban.* Good my lord, give me thy favour still.
Be patient, for the prize I'll bring thee to

Shall hoodwink this mischance: therefore speak softly.
All's hush'd as midnight yet.

*Trinculo.* Ay, but to lose our bottles in the pool,—

*Stephano.* There is not only disgrace and dishonour in that, monster, but an infinite loss.

*Trinculo.* That's more to me than my wetting: yet this is your harmless fairy, monster.

*Stephano.* I will fetch off my bottle, though I be o'er ears for my labour.

*Caliban.* Prithee, my king, be quiet. Seest thou here,
This is the mouth o' th' cell: no noise, and enter.
Do that good mischief which may make this island
Thine own for ever, and I, thy Caliban,
For aye thy foot-licker.

*Stephano.* Give me thy hand. I do begin to have bloody thoughts.

*Trinculo.* O King Stephano! O peer! O worthy Stephano! look what a wardrobe here is for thee!

*Caliban.* Let it alone, thou fool; it is but trash.

*Trinculo.* O, ho, monster! we know what belongs to a frippery.—O King Stephano!

*Stephano.* Put off that gown, Trinculo; by this hand,
I'll have that gown.

*Trinculo.* Thy grace shall have it.

*Caliban.* The dropsy drown this fool! What do you mean,
To dote thus on such luggage? Let's alone,
And do the murther first: if he awake,
From toe to crown he'll fill our skins with pinches,
Make us strange stuff.

*Stephano.* Be you quiet, monster.—Mistress line, is not this my jerkin? Now is the jerkin under the line: now, jerkin, you are like to lose your hair, and prove a bald jerkin.

*Trinculo.* Do, do: we steal by line and level, an't like your grace.

*Stephano.* I thank thee for that jest; here's a garment for't:

wit shall not go unrewarded while I am king of this country. "Steal by line and level" is an excellent pass of pate; there's another garment for't.

*Trinculo.* Monster, come, put some lime upon your fingers, and away with the rest.

*Caliban.* I will have none on't: we shall lose our time,
And all be turn'd to barnacles, or to apes
With foreheads villanous low.

*Stephano.* Monster, lay-to your fingers: help to bear this away where my hogshead of wine is, or I'll turn you out of my kingdom: go to, carry this.

*Trinculo.* And this.

*Stephano.* Ay, and this.

*A noise of hunters heard. Enter divers Spirits, in shape of dogs and hounds, and hunt them about,* PROSPERO *and* ARIEL *setting them on.*

*Prospero.* Hey, Mountain, hey!

*Ariel.* Silver! there it goes, Silver!

*Prospero.* Fury, Fury! there, Tyrant, there! hark, hark!
[*Caliban, Stephano, and Trinculo are driven out.*
Go charge my goblins that they grind their joints
With dry convulsions, shorten up their sinews
With aged cramps, and more pinch-spotted make them
Than pard or cat o' mountain.

*Ariel.* Hark, they roar!

*Prospero.* Let them be hunted soundly. At this hour
Lies at my mercy all mine enemies:
Shortly shall all my labours end, and thou
Shalt have the air at freedom. For a little
Follow, and do me service. [*Exeunt.*

## ACT V.

SCENE I. *Before the cell of Prospero.*

*Enter* PROSPERO *in his magic robes, and* ARIEL.

*Prospero.* Now does my project gather to a head:
My charms crack not, my spirits obey, and Time
Goes upright with his carriage. How's the day?

*Ariel.* On the sixth hour; at which time, my lord,
You said our work should cease.
*Prospero.* I did say so,
When first I rais'd the tempest. Say, my spirit,
How fares the king and's followers?
*Ariel.* Confin'd together
In the same fashion as you gave in charge,
Just as you left them; all prisoners, sir,
In the line-grove which weather-fends your cell;
They cannot budge till your release. The king,
His brother, and yours, abide all three distracted,
And the remainder mourning over them,
Brimful of sorrow and dismay; but chiefly
Him that you term'd, sir, the good old lord, Gonzalo;
His tears run down his beard, like winter's drops
From eaves of reeds. Your charm so strongly works 'em
That if you now beheld them, your affections
Would become tender.
*Prospero.* Dost thou think so, spirit
*Ariel.* Mine would, sir, were I human.
*Prospero.* And mine shall.
Hast thou, which art but air, a touch, a feeling
Of their afflictions, and shall not myself,
One of their kind, that relish all as sharply
Passion as they, be kindlier mov'd than thou art?
Though with their high wrongs I am struck to the quick,
Yet with my nobler reason 'gainst my fury
Do I take part. The rarer action is
In virtue than in vengeance: they being penitent,
The sole drift of my purpose doth extend
Not a frown further. Go release them, Ariel:
My charms I'll break, their senses I'll restore,
And they shall be themselves.
*Ariel.* I'll fetch them, sir. [*Exit.*
*Prospero.* Ye elves of hills, brooks, standing lakes, and groves;

And ye that on the sands with printless foot
Do chase the ebbing Neptune, and do fly him
When he comes back; you demi-puppets that
By moonshine do the green sour ringlets make,
Whereof the ewe not bites; and you whose pastime
Is to make midnight mushrooms, that rejoice
To hear the solemn curfew; by whose aid—
Weak masters though ye be—I have bedimm'd
The noontide sun, call'd forth the mutinous winds,
And 'twixt the green sea and the azur'd vault
Set roaring war: to the dread rattling thunder
Have I given fire, and rifted Jove's stout oak
With his own bolt; the strong-bas'd promontory
Have I made shake, and by the spurs pluck'd up
The pine and cedar: graves at my command
Have wak'd their sleepers, op'd, and let 'em forth
By my so potent art. But this rough magic
I here abjure; and, when I have requir'd
Some heavenly music—which even now I do,—
To work mine end upon their senses, that
This airy charm is for, I'll break my staff,
Bury it certain fathoms in the earth,
And deeper than did ever plummet sound
I'll drown my book. [*Solemn music.*

*Here enter* ARIEL *before: then* ALONSO, *with a frantic gesture, attended by* GONZALO; SEBASTIAN *and* ANTONIO *in like manner, attended by* ADRIAN *and* FRANCISCO: *they all enter the circle which* PROSPERO *had made, and there stand charmed; which* PROSPERO *observing, speaks:*

A solemn air, and the best comforter
To an unsettled fancy, cure thy brains,
Now useless, boil'd within thy skull! There stand,
For you are spell-stopp'd.—
Holy Gonzalo, honourable man,

Mine eyes, even sociable to the show of thine,
Fall fellowly drops.—The charm dissolves apace;
And as the morning steals upon the night,
Melting the darkness, so their rising senses
Begin to chase the ignorant fumes that mantle
Their clearer reason.—O good Gonzalo,
My true preserver, and a loyal sir
To him thou follow'st! I will pay thy graces
Home both in word and deed. Most cruelly
Didst thou, Alonso, use me and my daughter:
Thy brother was a furtherer in the act;—
Thou art pinch'd for't now, Sebastian.—Flesh and blood,
You, brother mine, that entertain'd ambition,
Expell'd remorse and nature; who, with Sebastian,—
Whose inward pinches therefore are most strong,—
Would here have kill'd your king; I do forgive thee,
Unnatural though thou art.—Their understanding
Begins to swell; and the approaching tide
Will shortly fill the reasonable shore,
That now lies foul and muddy. Not one of them
That yet looks on me, or would know me.—Ariel,
Fetch me the hat and rapier in my cell:
I will discase me, and myself present
As I was sometime Milan. Quickly, spirit;
Thou shalt ere long be free.

ARIEL *sings, and helps to attire him.*

*Where the bee sucks, there suck I:*
*In a cowslip's bell I lie;*
*There I couch when owls do cry.*
*On the bat's back I do fly*
*After summer merrily.*
*Merrily, merrily, shall I live now*
*Under the blossom that hangs on the bough.*

*Prospero.* Why, that's my dainty Ariel! I shall miss thee;
But yet thou shalt have freedom:—so, so, so.—
To the king's ship, invisible as thou art:
There shalt thou find the mariners asleep
Under the hatches; the master and the boatswain
Being awake, enforce them to this place,
And presently, I prithee.
*Ariel.* I drink the air before me, and return
Or ere your pulse twice beat. [*Exit.*
*Gonzalo.* All torment, trouble, wonder, and amazement
Inhabits here: some heavenly power guide us
Out of this fearful country!
*Prospero.* Behold, Sir King,
The wronged Duke of Milan, Prospero:
For more assurance that a living prince
Does now speak to thee, I embrace thy body;
And to thee and thy company I bid
A hearty welcome.
*Alonso.* Whe'r thou beest he or no,
Or some enchanted trifle to abuse me,
As late I have been, I not know: thy pulse
Beats, as of flesh and blood; and, since I saw thee,
Th' affliction of my mind amends, with which,
I fear, a madness held me. This must crave—
An if this be at all—a most strange story.
Thy dukedom I resign, and do entreat
Thou pardon me my wrongs.—But how should Prospero
Be living and be here?
*Prospero.* First, noble friend,
Let me embrace thine age, whose honour cannot
Be measur'd or confin'd.
*Gonzalo.* Whether this be
Or be not, I'll not swear.
*Prospero.* You do yet taste

Some subtleties o' th' isle, that will not let you
Believe things certain.—Welcome, my friends all !—
[*Aside to Sebastian and Antonio.*] But you, my brace of lords,
were I so minded,
I here could pluck his highness' frown upon you,
And justify you traitors : at this time
I'll tell no tales.

*Sebastian* [*Aside*]. The devil speaks in him.

*Prospero.* No.—
For you, most wicked sir, whom to call brother
Would even infect my mouth, I do forgive
Thy rankest fault,—all of them ; and require
My dukedom of thee, which perforce I know
Thou must restore.

*Alonso.* If thou beest Prospero,
Give us particulars of thy preservation :
How thou hast met us here, whom three hours since
Were wrack'd upon this shore ; where I have lost—
How sharp the point of this remembrance is !—
My dear son Ferdinand.

*Prospero.* I am woe for't, sir.

*Alonso.* Irreparable is the loss ; and patience
Says it is past her cure.

*Prospero.* I rather think
You have not sought her help ; of whose soft grace
For the like loss I have her sovereign aid,
And rest myself content.

*Alonso.* You the like loss ?

*Prospero.* As great to me as late ; and supportable
To make the dear loss have I means much weaker
Than you may call to comfort you, for I
Have lost my daughter.

*Alonso.* A daughter ?
O heavens, that they were living both in Naples,
The king and queen there ! that they were, I wish

Myselı were mudded in that oozy bed
Where my son lies. When did you lose your daughter?
*Prospero.* In this last tempest. I perceive, these lords
At this encounter do so much admire,
That they devour their reason, and scarce think
Their eyes do offices of truth, their words
Are natural breath: but, howsoe'er you have
Been justled from your senses, know for certain
That I am Prospero, and that very duke
Which was thrust forth of Milan; who most strangely
Upon this shore, where you were wrack'd, was landed,
To be the lord on't. No more yet of this;
For 'tis a chronicle of day by day,
Not a relation for a breakfast, nor
Befitting this first meeting. Welcome, sir;
This cell's my court: here have I few attendants,
And subjects none abroad: pray you, look in.
My dukedom since you have given me again,
I will requite you with as good a thing;
At least bring forth a wonder, to content ye
As much as me my dukedom.

*Here* PROSPERO *discovers* FERDINAND *and* MIRANDA *playing at chess.*

*Miranda.* Sweet lord, you play me false.
*Ferdinand.* No, my dearest love,
I would not for the world.
*Miranda.* Yes, for a score of kingdoms you should wrangle,
And I would call it fair play.
*Alonso.* If this prove
A vision of the island, one dear son
Shall I twice lose.
*Sebastian.* A most high miracle!
*Ferdinand.* Though the seas threaten, they are merciful;
I have curs'd them without cause. [*Kneels.*

*Alonso.* Now all the blessings
Of a glad father compass thee about!
Arise, and say how thou cam'st here.
*Miranda.* O, wonder!
How many goodly creatures are there here!
How beauteous mankind is! O brave new world,
That has such people in't!
*Prospero.* 'Tis new to thee.
*Alonso.* What is this maid with whom thou wast at play?
Your eld'st acquaintance cannot be three hours:
Is she the goddess that hath sever'd us,
And brought us thus together?
*Ferdinand.* Sir, she is mortal;
But by immortal Providence she's mine:
I chose her when I could not ask my father
For his advice, nor thought I had one. She
Is daughter to this famous Duke of Milan,
Of whom so often I have heard renown,
But never saw before; of whom I have
Receiv'd a second life, and second father
This lady makes him to me.
*Alonso.* I am hers.
But, O, how oddly will it sound, that I
Must ask my child forgiveness!
*Prospero.* There, sir, stop:
Let us not burthen our remembrances
With a heaviness that's gone.
*Gonzalo.* I have inly wept,
Or should have spoke ere this. Look down, you gods,
And on this couple drop a blessed crown!
For it is you that have chalk'd forth the way
Which brought us hither.
*Alonso.* I say Amen, Gonzalo!
*Gonzalo.* Was Milan thrust from Milan, that his issue
Should become kings of Naples? O, rejoice

Beyond a common joy! and set it down
With gold on lasting pillars:—In one voyage
Did Claribel her husband find at Tunis;
And Ferdinand her brother found a wife,
Where he himself was lost; Prospero his dukedom,
In a poor isle; and all of us ourselves,
When no man was his own.

*Alonso* [*to Ferdinand and Miranda*]. Give me your hands:
Let grief and sorrow still embrace his heart
That doth not wish you joy!

*Gonzalo.* Be it so! Amen!

*Enter* ARIEL, *with the* Master *and* Boatswain *amazedly following.*

O, look, sir! look, sir! here is more of us:
I prophesied, if a gallows were on land,
This fellow could not drown.—Now, blasphemy,
That swear'st grace o'erboard, not an oath on shore?
Hast thou no mouth by land? What is the news?

*Boatswain.* The best news is, that we have safely found
Our king and company; the next, our ship—
Which, but three glasses since, we gave out split—
Is tight, and yare, and bravely rigg'd as when
We first put out to sea.

*Ariel* [*Aside to Prospero*]. Sir, all this service
Have I done since I went.

*Prospero* [*Aside to Ariel*]. My tricksy spirit!

*Alonso.* These are not natural events; they strengthen
From strange to stranger.—Say, how came you hither?

*Boatswain.* If I did think, sir, I were well awake,
I'd strive to tell you. We were dead of sleep,
And—how we know not—all clapp'd under hatches;
Where, but even now, with strange and several noises
Of roaring, shrieking, howling, jingling chains,
And more diversity of sounds, all horrible,

We were awak'd ; straightway, at liberty ;
Where we, in all her trim, freshly beheld
Our royal, good, and gallant ship ; our master
Capering to eye her. On a trice, so please you,
Even in a dream, were we divided from them
And were brought moping hither.

*Ariel* [*Aside to Prospero*]. Was't well done?

*Prospero* [*Aside to Ariel*]. Bravely, my diligence. Thou shalt be free.

*Alonso.* This is as strange a maze as e'er men trod ;
And there is in this business more than nature
Was ever conduct of: some oracle
Must rectify our knowledge.

*Prospero.* Sir, my liege,
Do not infest your mind with beating on
The strangeness of this business. At pick'd leisure,
Which shall be shortly, single I'll resolve you,
Which to you shall seem probable, of every
These happen'd accidents ; till when, be cheerful,
And think of each thing well. [*Aside to Ariel.*] Come hither, spirit:
Set Caliban and his companions free ;
Untie the spell. [*Exit Ariel.*] How fares my gracious sir?
There are yet missing of your company
Some few odd lads that you remember not.

*Enter* ARIEL, *driving in* CALIBAN, STEPHANO, *and* TRINCULO, *in their stolen apparel.*

*Stephano.* Every man shift for all the rest, and let no man take care for himself, for all is but fortune.—Coragio, bully-monster, coragio!

*Trinculo.* If these be true spies which I wear in my head, here's a goodly sight.

*Caliban.* O Setebos, these be brave spirits indeed!
How fine my master is! I am afraid
He will chastise me.

*Sebastian.* Ha, ha!
What things are these, my lord Antonio?
Will money buy 'em?

*Antonio.* Very like; one of them
Is a plain fish, and, no doubt, marketable.

*Prospero.* Mark but the badges of these men, my lords,
Then say if they be true.—This misshapen knave,
His mother was a witch; and one so strong
That could control the moon, make flows and ebbs,
And deal in her command without her power.
These three have robb'd me; and this demi-devil—
For he's a bastard one—had plotted with them
To take my life. Two of these fellows you
Must know and own; this thing of darkness I
Acknowledge mine.

*Caliban.* I shall be pinch'd to death.

*Alonso.* Is not this Stephano, my drunken butler?

*Sebastian.* He is drunk now: where had he wine?

*Alonso.* And Trinculo is reeling ripe: where should they
Find this grand liquor that hath gilded 'em?
How cam'st thou in this pickle?

*Trinculo.* I have been in such a pickle, since I saw you last, that, I fear me, will never out of my bones: I shall not fear fly-blowing.

*Sebastian.* Why, how now, Stephano!

*Stephano.* O, touch me not; I am not Stephano, but a cramp.

*Prospero.* You'd be king o' the isle, sirrah?

*Stephano.* I should have been a sore one, then.

*Alonso.* This is a strange thing as e'er I look'd on.
[*Pointing to Caliban.*

*Prospero.* He is as disproportion'd in his manners
As in his shape.—Go, sirrah, to my cell;
Take with you your companions; as you look
To have my pardon, trim it handsomely.

*Caliban.* Ay, that I will; and I'll be wise hereafter,
And seek for grace. What a thrice-double ass
Was I, to take this drunkard for a god,
And worship this dull fool!

*Prospero.* Go to; away!

*Alonso.* Hence, and bestow your luggage where you found it.

*Sebastian.* Or stole it, rather.

[*Exeunt Caliban, Stephano, and Trinculo.*

*Prospero.* Sir, I invite your highness and your train
To my poor cell, where you shall take your rest
For this one night; which, part of it, I'll waste
With such discourse as, I not doubt, shall make it
Go quick away,—the story of my life,
And the particular accidents gone by
Since I came to this isle: and in the morn
I'll bring you to your ship, and so to Naples,
Where I have hope to see the nuptial
Of these our dear-belov'd solemnized;
And thence retire me to my Milan, where
Every third thought shall be my grave.

*Alonso.* I long
To hear the story of your life, which must
Take the ear strangely.

*Prospero.* I'll deliver all;
And promise you calm seas, auspicious gales,
And sail so expeditious that shall catch
Your royal fleet far off. [*Aside to Ariel.*] My Ariel, chick,
That is thy charge: then to the elements
Be free, and fare thou well!—Please you, draw near.

[*Exeunt.*

## EPILOGUE.

SPOKEN BY PROSPERO.

[Now my charms are all o'erthrown,
And what strength I have's mine own,
Which is most faint: now, 'tis true,
I must be here confin'd by you,
Or sent to Naples. Let me not,
Since I have my dukedom got,
And pardon'd the deceiver, dwell
In this bare island by your spell;
But release me from my bands
With the help of your good hands:
Gentle breath of yours my sails
Must fill, or else my project fails,
Which was to please. Now I want
Spirits to enforce, art to enchant;
And my ending is despair,
Unless I be reliev'd by prayer;
Which pierces so that it assaults
Mercy itself, and frees all faults.
As you from crimes would pardon'd be,
Let your indulgence set me free.]

# NOTES.

## ABBREVIATIONS USED IN THE NOTES.

Abbott (or Gr.), Abbott's *Shakespearian Grammar*.
A. S., Anglo-Saxon.
B. and F., Beaumont and Fletcher.
C., Craik's *English of Shakespeare* (Rolfe's edition).
Cf. (*confer*), compare.
Com., Milton's *Comus*.
D., Dyce.
F., Fowler's *English Language* (8vo edition).
F. Q., Spenser's *Faërie Queene*.
Foll., following.
Fr., French.
H., Hudson.
Id. (*idem*), the same.
Il Pens., Milton's *Il Penseroso*.
K., Knight.
Mer., Rolfe's edition of *The Merchant of Venice*.
N. F., Norman French.
P. L., Milton's *Paradise Lost*.
Phila. ed., Notes of Studies on *The Tempest*, by Shakespeare Society of Phila.
Prol., Prologue.
Rich., Richardson's Dictionary (London, 1838).
S., Shakespeare
Shep. Cal., Spenser's *Shepherd's Calendar*.
Sr., Singer.
St., Staunton.
V., Verplanck.
Var. ed., the *Variorum* edition of Shakespeare (1821).
W., White.
Wb., Webster's Dictionary (revised quarto edition of 1864).
Worc., Worcester's Dictionary (quarto edition).

The abbreviations of the names of Shakespeare's Plays will be readily understood; as *T. N.* for *Twelfth Night*, *Cor.* for *Coriolanus*, 3 *Hen. VI.* for *The Third Part of King Henry the Sixth*, etc. *P. P.* refers to *The Passionate Pilgrim*; *V. and A.* to *Venus and Adonis*; *L. C.* to *A Lover's Complaint*; and *Sonn.* to the *Sonnets*.

# NOTES.

## ACT I.

SCENE I.—In the first folio, the play is divided into acts and scenes. At the end, printed side by side with the Epilogue, a list of *dramatis personæ* is given, under the heading "*Names of the Actors*," and above this is "The Scene, an vn-inhabited Island."

*What cheer?* On *cheer*, see *Mer.* p. 152.

*Good, speak to th' mariners.* That is, good *boatswain* or *fellow*, as D., W., and others explain it. The folio has "Good: Speake to th' Mariners:" and H. and others retain that pointing, making *good*=good *cheer.* But the cheer was *not* good, as they were running aground. Cf. also just below, "Nay, good, be patient," and *Ham.* i. 1: "Good now, sit down."

*Yarely.* Readily, nimbly; from *yare*, quick, active. · Cf. *T. N.* iii. 4: "be yare in thy preparation;" *M. for M.* iv. 2: "you shall find me yare " *A. and C.* v. 2: "Yare, yare, good Iras, quick," etc. So in Chaucer, *Legend of Good Women*, 2268: "This Tereus let make hys shippes yare;" that is, had his ships made ready.

*Cheerly.* An example of "*-ly* found with a noun, and yet not appearing to convey an adjectival meaning." Gr. 447. Cf. "angerly," *Macb.* iii. 5; "hungerly," *Oth.* iii. 4, etc. S. uses *cheerly* often, but *cheerily* not once. Rich. gives an example of the latter from B. and F. Milton has *cheerly* in *L'Allegro*—the only instance in which he uses either.

*Tend.* Attend, as often. Cf. *Rich. III.* iv. 1: "Good angels tend thee!" *Lear*, ii. 1: "knights that tend upon my father," etc.

*If room enough.* If there be sea-room enough. Cf. *Per.* iii. 1: "But sea-room, and (an) the brine and cloudy billows kiss the moon, I care not."

*Play the men.* Play the part of men; behave like men. Cf. 2 *Sam.* x. 12. See also Chapman's *Iliad*, bk. v.:—

"Which doing, thou shalt know what souldiers play the men,
And what the cowards."

And Marlowe's *Tamburlaine*, i. 1: "Viceroys and peers of Turkey, play the men."

*Where is the master, boatswain?* The folio has "Boson," which W. retains; but his reasons for it are hardly satisfactory.

*You do assist the storm.* Cf. *Per.* iii. 1: "Patience, good sir; do not assist the storm."

*What cares these roarers*, etc. H. and others change *cares* to *care*, but *cares* is probably an example of the old plural in *-s*. See *Mer.* p. 136 (note on *Dealings teaches them suspect*) and Gr. 333. Of course no typographical error is possible in cases where the *rhyme* requires the form in *-s*; as

"There lies
Two kinsmen digg'd their graves with weeping eyes."
*Rich. II.* iii. 3.

"She lifts the coffer-lids that close his eyes,
Where lo! two lamps burnt out in darkness lies."
*V. and A.* 1128.

"Those petty wrongs that liberty commits
Thy beauty and thy years full well befits."
*Sonnet* 41.

"And to their audit comes
Their distract parcels in combined sums."
*L. C.* 230.

*To cabin.* Abbott (Gr. 90) gives many similar examples of the omission of *the*; as "At door" (*W. T.* iv. 4, and *T. of S.* iv. 1), "At end" (*Cor.* iv. 7), "To west" (*Sonn.* 33), etc.

*Of the present.* Cf. *J. C.* i. 2: "For this present," and 1 *Cor.* xv. 6.

*Methinks.* See *Mer.* p. 135, note on *Methought.*

*He hath no drowning mark upon him*, etc. The allusion to the familiar proverb is obvious. Cf. *T. G. of V.* i. 1:—

"Go, go, begone to save your ship from wrack,
Which cannot perish having thee aboard,
Being destin'd to a drier death on shore."

*Down with the topmast*, etc. Striking the topmast was a new invention in S.'s time, which he here very properly introduces. Lord Mulgrave, who shows that this whole scene is "a very striking instance of the great accuracy of S.'s knowledge in a professional science, the most difficult to attain without the help of experience," explains this manœuvre as follows: "The gale encreasing, the topmast is struck to take the weight from aloft, make the ship drive less to leeward, and bear the mainsail under which the ship is laid to." *Lower* is in the imperative mood.

*Bring her to try wi' th' main course.* Malone quotes Hakluyt's *Voyages* (1598): "And when the barke had way, we cut the hauser, and so gate the sea to our friend, and tried out all that day with our maine course."

The phrase is also found in Smith's *Sea-Grammar*, 1627. The folio reads, "bring her to Try with Maine-course;" and W. thinks it should be pointed thus: "Bring her to: try wi' th' main course."

*I'll warrant him for drowning.* *For* here may be either "as regards" or "against." Examples of the latter meaning are:—

> "Somme shal sowe the sakke, quod Piers, for shedyng of the whete."
> *Piers the Plowman's Vision*, vi. 9.

> "And next his schert an aketoun,
> And over that an haberjoun,
> For persying of his hert."
> Chaucer, *Sir Thopas*.

> "We'll have a bib for spoiling of thy doublet."
> B. and F., *Captain*, iii. 5.

> "If he were too long for the bed, they cut off his legs, for catching cold."
> Lyly, *Euphues*.

*Lay her a-hold, a-hold.* To lay a ship a-hold is to bring her to lie as near to the wind as she can, in order to keep clear of the land, and get her out to sea. [Steevens.]

*Set her two courses.* That is, the mainsail ("the main course," above) and foresail. The folio reads: "Lay her a hold, a hold, set her two courses off to Sea againe, lay her off," and some modern editors put no point after "courses."

*Must our mouths be cold?* Must we die? It has been suggested (Phila. ed.) that it may mean, Must we resort to cowardly prayers? and the following from B. and F. (*Sea Voyage*, i. 1, an imitation of *The Tempest*) is cited in support of the explanation:—

> "Thou rascal, thou fearful rogue, thou hast been *praying:*
> ——————is this a time
> To discourage our friends with your *cold orisons?*"

*We are merely cheated*, etc. Absolutely cheated. Cf. "mere enemy," *M. of V.* iii. 2; "the mere perdition (that is, the entire destruction) of the Turkish fleet," *Oth.* ii. 2; "the mere undoing (the complete ruin) of all the kingdom," *Hen. VIII.* iii. 2; etc. So in Bacon's 58th *Essay:* "As for conflagrations and great droughts, they do not merely (that is, entirely) dispeople and destroy;" where most of the modern editors (Montague and Whately included), mistaking the meaning, have changed "*and* destroy" to "*but* destroy."

*To glut him.* To swallow him. Cf. Milton, *P. L.* x. 633: "sucked and glutted offal."

*Long heath, brown furze.* Hanmer suggested "ling, heath, broom, furze," which D. adopts; but there seems no good reason for altering the text of the folio.

SCENE II.—*Mounting to the welkin's cheek.* Cf. *Rich. II.* iii. 3:—

> "Their thundering shock
> At meeting tears the cloudy cheeks of heaven."

*Who had no doubt some noble creature in her.* On *who*=*which*, see *Mer.* p. 144 (note on *Of gold, who*) and Gr. 264. D., St., and some others change *creature* to *creatures.*

*Or ere.* The *or* is undoubtedly the A. S. *ær* (our *ere*) which appears in early English in the forms *er*, *air*, *ar*, *ear*, *or*, *eror*. We find *or*=*before* in Chaucer, as in the *Knightes Tale*, 1685: "Cleer was the day, as I have told or this;" and later, as in Latimer and Ascham. *Ere* seems to have been added to *or* for emphasis when the meaning of the latter was dying out. In early English we find such combinations as *erst er*, *bifore er*, *before or* (Mätzner, iii. 451).

Some explain *or ere*, which they write *or e'er*, as a contraction of *or ever* =before ever. *Or ever* is, indeed, not unfrequently found (in the Bible, for instance, in *Eccles.* xii. 6; *Prov.* viii. 23; *Dan.* vi. 24, etc.); but, as Abbott remarks (Gr. 131), it is much more likely that *ever* should be substituted for *ere* than *ere* for *ever*.

*Fraughting.* Making up her *fraught*, or freight. S. does not use *freight*, either as a verb or a noun. See note on *fraught*, in *Mer.* p. 145.

*More better.* For other examples of double comparatives and superlatives in S., see *Mer.* p. 159 (note on *more elder*), and Gr. 11.

*Full poor cell.* *Full*=to the full, very. Cf. "full sorry," *A. and C.* i. 1, etc.

*Meddle with my thoughts.* That is, *mingle* with them. Cf. Wiclif, *Matt.* xxvii. 24: "wyn medlid with gall;" *John*, xix. 39: "a medling of myrre and aloes;" Chaucer, *Legend of Good Women*, 874:

"How medeleth she his blood with hir compleynte?"

Spenser, *Shep. Cal. Apr.* 68:

"The redde rose medled with the white yfere;"

Hooker, *Eccl. Pol.* iv. 8: "A meddled estate of the orders of the Gospel and the ceremonies of poperie;" etc.

*Lie there my art.* Fuller (*Holy State*, iv. 6) says that Lord Burleigh, when he put off his gown at night, used to say, "Lie there, Lord Treasurer."

*The direful spectacle of the wrack.* The word is invariably *wrack* in S. In *Lucrece* we have it rhyming with *back*.

*The very virtue of compassion.* The very essence or soul of it.

*I have with such provision.* Hunter suggested *prevision*, which D. adopts; but, as Mrs. Kemble remarks (*Atlantic Monthly*, vol. viii. p. 290), "It is very true that *pre*vision means the foresight that his art gave him, but *pro*vision implies the exercise of that foresight or *pre*vision; it is therefore better, because more comprehensive."

*So safely ordered that there is no soul—* This is quite obviously an instance of anacoluthon, but Theo. proposed *no foil*, and Pope followed him. Capell read *no loss*; Rowe and Warburton, *no soul lost.* Johnson suggested *no soil.*

*Betid.* The *-ed* of the participle is often omitted after *d* and *t.* Gr. 342. Thus we have *acquit* (*Rich. III.* v. 5), *bloat* (*Ham.* iii. 4), *enshield* (*M. for M.* ii. 4), etc. A few lines below we have "The very rats instinctively have *quit* it."

*Out three years old.* *Out*=past, more than. Nares explains it as "completely." Cf. "Be a boy right out," iv. 1. See Gr. 183.

*Twelve year since*, etc. The folio reads, "Twelue yere since (*Miranda*), twelue yere since." Pope needlessly changed *year* to *years*, and some recent editors have followed him.

*And his only heir*, etc. The reading of the folio is,

> "Was Duke of *Millaine*, and his onely heire,
> And Princesse; no worse Issued."

With a slight change in the pointing this is clear enough, but Hanmer made it read

> "Was Duke of Milan; thou his only heir
> And princess, no worse issued."

Pope then changed "And princess" to "A princess." D. adopts both emendations.

*Holp.* For *holpen*, the old participle of *help.* For the full form see *Ps.* lxxxiii. 8; *Dan.* xi. 34, etc. The contracted form is common in early writers; as in *Piers the Plowman's Vision*, iv. 169: "For ofte haue I, quod he, holpe you atte barre." *Holp* is properly the past tense of *help*, and S. uses it as such in *Cor.* v. 3: "I holp to frame thee;" *Lear*, iii. 7: "he holp the heavens to rain;" etc. He uses *holp* (and *holp'st*) nineteen times, and *helped* (as past tense and participle) only six times.

*Teen.* Grief, trouble. Cf. *R. and J.* i. 3: "to my teen be it spoken;" *L. L. L.* iv. 3: "of groans, of sorrow, and of teen;" etc. Also, Spenser, *F. Q.* i. 9, 34: "for dread and dolefull teen;" *Shep. Cal. Nov.* 41: "my woful teen;" etc.

*Which is from my remembrance.* That is, away from. Often so used; as *J. C.* i. 3: "clean from the purpose;" *T. N.* i. 5: "This is from my commission;" etc. See Gr. 158.

*My brother and thy uncle*, etc. This, with the following speech of Prospero, has well been called "a network of anacolutha." "The subject, *My brother*, is dropped, and taken up again as *he whom*, and finally in *false uncle*, before its verb (but only after another interruption) is reached in *new created.* A parenthesis begins with *as at that time;* but it ceases to be treated as a parenthesis, and eddies into the main current of expression at *These being all my study*" (Phila. ed.).

*Manage.* See *Mer.* p. 153.

*As at that time.* The *as* is probably redundant here, as it often is in statements of time. In early English *as* is often prefixed to dates: "as this year of grace," etc. Chaucer has *as now, as here*, etc.=*now, here*, etc. Prof. G. Allen (Phila. ed.), who was the first to call attention to this use of *as* in S., quotes the Collect for Christmas in the Prayer-Book: "Almighty God, who hast given us thy only-begotten Son to take our nature upon him, and *as at this time* to be born," etc. See also Gr. 114. Cf. *M. for M.* v. 1: "One Lucio *as then* the messenger."

*Through all the signiories it was the first.* Botero (*Relations of the World*, 1630) says, "Milan claims to be the first duchy in Europe."

*Who t' advance, and who*, etc. On *who=whom*, see *Mer.* pp. 131, 143, and Gr. 274.

*To trash for overtopping.* A metaphor taken from hunting. To *trash* a hound was to check or hamper him, so that he would not *overtop* or outrun the pack. Cf. *Oth.* ii. 1:

"If this poor trash of Venice, whom I *trash*
For his quick hunting."

For another explanation, see note on the passage in *Var.* edit., or Dyce's *Glossary* under *trash.*

*That now he was.* So that now he was; a common ellipsis. Gr. 283.

*The ivy,* etc. The ivy was thought to be a parasitic plant and injurious to trees. Cf. *C. of E.* ii. 2: "usurping ivy."

*Out on't.* See *Mer.* p. 143, and Gr. 182.

*Closeness.* Privacy, seclusion. Cf. the use of *close* and *closely;* as, "a close (secret) exploit of death" (*Rich. III.* iv. 2); "we have closely (privately) sent for Hamlet" (*Ham.* iii. 1), etc.

*But by being so retir'd.* "Were it only for the retirement it procured me;" or, perhaps, *except for* its being so retired.

*Like a good parent.* "Alluding to the observation that a father above the common rate of men has commonly a son below it. *Heroum filii noxae*" (Johnson).

*Sans bound.* Without limit. As Nares remarks, "a general combination seems to have subsisted, among all our poets, to introduce this French word, certainly very convenient for their verse, into the English language; but in vain; the country never received it, and it has always appeared as an exotic, even though the elder poets Anglicized its form into *saunce,* or gave it the English pronunciation." In a familiar passage in *A. Y. L.* (ii. 7), S. uses it four times in a single line. Cf. also *L. L. L.* v. 2:

"My love to thee is sound, sans crack or flaw.
*Rosalind.* Sans sans, I pray you."

*Lorded.* Made a lord. Cf. *strangered*=made a stranger (*Lear,* i. 1), and *servanted*=made subservient (*Cor.* v. 2). But *kinged*=ruled (*K. John,* ii. 1), *fathered*=provided with a father (*J. C.* ii. 1, and *Lear,* iii. 6), *lovered*=gifted with a lover (*L. C.*), etc. See Gr. 294.

*Revenue.* The accent on the penult, as in *Ham.* iii. 2: "from thee that no revenue hast," and *M. N. D.* i. 1: "Of great revenue, and she hath no child;" but in the same scene of *M. N. D.* we find it with the modern accent: "Long withering out a young man's revenue." For a list of words used by S. with "the accent nearer the end than with us," see Gr. 490; but *revenue* is omitted.

*Like one Who unto truth,* etc. The folio has *into* truth, which D. retains, quoting as another instance of *into* for *unto,* "And pray God's blessing into thy attempt," *A. W.* i. 3. In "telling of it," *it* refers to *lie,* by anticipation. *As* is omitted before "To credit." Cf. "so fond to come abroad," *M. of V.* iii. 3; "so big to hold so much," *T. N.* ii. 4, etc. Gr. 281.

*Dost thou hear?* On S.'s use of *thou* and *you,* see Gr. 231–235.

*He needs will be.* On *needs,* see *Mer.* p. 141, and Gr. 25.

*Me, poor man!* As for me. D. says, "*For* me . . . large enough," and compares *T. of A.* v. 1:—

"Whose thankless natures—O abhorred spirits!—
Not all the whips of heaven are large enough," etc.

*If this might be a brother.* Examples of *might* in the sense of *could* are not uncommon. Cf. *M. N. D.* ii. 1: "But I might see young Cupid's fiery shaft," etc.; *Ham.* i. 1:—

> "I might not this believe
> Without the sensible and true avouch
> Of mine own eyes."

For other examples, see Gr. 312.

*To think but nobly.* That is, *otherwise than* nobly. Gr. 124.

*Hearkens my brother's suit.* Cf. 2 *Hen. IV.* ii. 4: "Hearken the end." Gr. 199.

*In lieu o' th' premises.* That is, in consideration of. Cf. "in lieu thereof" (*T. G. of V.* ii. 7, and *L. L. L.* iii. 1), "in lieu whereof" (*K. John*, v. 4), etc.

*It is a hint.* A cause, or subject. Cf. "our hint of woe," ii. 1.

*Without the which.* See *Mer.* p. 133 (note on *For the which*), and Gr. 270.

*Were most impertinent.* Cf. *Lear*, iv. 6:—

> "O matter and impertinency mixed!
> Reason in madness!"

*Wench.* This word "originally meant young woman only, without the contemptuous familiarity now annexed to it." Cf. *Hen. VIII.* iv. 2: "When I am dead, good wench," etc.; *Oth.* v. 2: "O, ill-starred wench!" etc.

*In few.* In short. Cf. *Ham.* i. 3: "in few, Ophelia," etc. Gr. 5.

*Have quit it.* The reading of the folio, changed to *had* by D. and others. For *quit*, see above on *betid.* *Hoist* is a similar contraction. See Gr. 341, 342.

*Did us but loving wrong.* Jephson says, "that is, were merciful to us;" but I understand it to mean, "only injured us by their sympathetic sighing," that is, blowing.

*A cherubin.* This is the reading of the folio here, as well as in *T. of A.* iv. 3, *Macb.* i. 7, and *Oth.* iv. 2, the only other places in which S. uses the singular, except *Ham.* iv. 3, where *cherub* ("Cherube" in folio) occurs. He uses *cherubins* as the plural in *M. of V.* v. 1 (see *Mer.* p. 162), *Hen. VIII.* i. 1, *T. and C.* iii. 2, and *Cymb.* ii. 4. Neither *cherubim* nor *cherubims* is to be found in the folio, though both are given in most modern editions and in Mrs. Clarke's *Concordance.* In this passage H. has *cherubim*, but D. and W. *cherubin.*

*Deck'd.* "Here deck'd would appear to be a form, if it be not a corruption, of the provincialism *degg'd*, i. e. *sprinkled.*" (D.) Some editors have changed the word to *degg'd.*

*An undergoing stomach.* A sustaining courage. Cf. 2 *Hen. IV.* i. 1: "Gan vail his stomach" (began to let his courage sink), and *Ham.* i. 1: "some enterprise That hath a stomach in't" (that requires courage). Elsewhere it means anger, resentment, as in *T. G. of V.* i. 2: "kill your stomach on your meat;" and pride, arrogance, as in *Hen. VIII.* iv. 2: "He was a man of an unbounded stomach."

*Have steaded much.* Have been of much service. See *Mer.* p. 133, note on *Can you stead me?*

*But ever see that man.* But see that man at any time. Gr. 39.

*Now I arise.* It is very doubtful what this means. The stage direction, *Puts on his robe*, or *Resumes his robe*, given in some editions, is not found in the folio, but is due to Mr. Collier's MS. corrector. St. suggests that the words are spoken aside to Ariel, and quotes in support of that view the conclusion of Prospero's next speech, "Come away, servant, come! I'm ready now," etc.

*Made thee more profit Than other princess can. Profit* is here a verb. *Princess* (the reading of the folio) is here for *princesses*. As Abbott (Gr. 471) has shown, "the plural and possessive cases of nouns of which the singular ends in *s*, *se*, *ss*, *ce*, and *ge*, are frequently written, and still more frequently pronounced, without the additional syllable." Cf. *Macb.* v. 1 (folio): "Their *sense* are shut;" *Hen. V.* v. 2: "Your *mightiness* on both parts best can witness," etc. W. adopts Rowe's emendation of "princes," and gives quotations to show that "women as well as men of royal or ducal birth were called *prince* in S.'s day." But S. himself does not use *prince* for *princess*, while it is evident that he does drop the *-es* or *'s* in not a few such words. D. gives "princess'," and H. "princess."

*Now my dear lady.* Now friendly to me; or, as Steevens puts it, "now my auspicious mistress."

*I find my zenith*, etc. Cf. *J. C.* iv. 3: "There is a tide in the affairs of men," etc.

*Thou art inclin'd to sleep.* It is not easy to decide whether Miranda is put to sleep by the art of Prospero, or falls asleep from the effect of the strange things she has seen and heard. The latter view is well put by Franz Horn, who says: "The wonderful acts occasionally like the music upon Jessica in the fifth act of *The Merchant of Venice*. The external miracles of nature scarcely affect Miranda upon an island where nature itself has become a wonder, and the wonders have become nature. But for her, even on that account, there are only so many greater wonders in the heart and life of man. . . . The checkered course of the world, its wild passions, are to her wholly strange; and the relation of such wonders might well affect her in the manner her father fears."

*To answer thy best pleasure; be't to fly*, etc. Henley quotes the imitation of this passage by Fletcher, in *The Faithful Shepherdess*:—

> "Tell me, sweetest,
> What new service now is meetest
> For the satyre; shall I stray
> In the middle ayre, and stay
> The sailing rack, or nimbly take
> Hold by the moone, and gently make
> Suit to the pale queene of night,
> For a beame to give thee light?
> Shall I dive into the sea,
> And bring thee coral, making way
> Through the rising waves," etc.

*Ariel and all his quality.* That is, all his ability, his powers. D. explains it as "all those occupied in similar services, all his fellows."

*Perform'd to point.* Exactly, to the minutest point; like the French *à point.* See Gr. 187.

*The waist.* "That part of a ship which is contained between the quarter-deck and the forecastle." (Falconer's *Marine Dictionary.*)

*I'd divide.* *Will* and *would* are sometimes used to express a *repeated* or *customary* action. Gr. 330. Cf. *Oth.* i. 3: "But still the house affairs would draw her hence;" and below, iii. 2: "Sometimes a thousand twangling instruments Will hum about mine ears." So in Gray's *Elegy:* "His listless length at noontide would he stretch," etc.

*Distinctly.* In its original sense of *separately.* An allusion to the electrical phenomenon known as *Saint Elmo's fire.* In Hakluyt's *Voyages* (1598) there is the following description of it, which S. may have had in mind: "I do remember that in the great and boysterous storme of this foule weather, in the night there came upon the toppe of our maine yard and maine-mast a certaine little light, much like unto the light of a little candle, which the Spaniards call the *Cuerpo Santo.* This light continued aboord our ship about three houres, flying from maste to maste, and from top to top; and sometimes it would be in two or three places at once."

*Coil.* Turmoil, tumult. Cf. *T. of A.* i. 2: "what a coil's here!" *R. and J.* ii. 5: "here's such a coil!" etc.

*Fever of the mad.* Fever of delirium.

*Afire.* See Gr. 24.

*With hair up-staring.* See Gr. 429. Cf. *J. C.* iv. 3: "That makest my blood cold and my hair to stare."

*Their sustaining garments.* Bearing or resisting the effects of the water. Some explain it as "bearing them up in the water."

*Cooling of the air.* See Gr. 178. Cf. 3 *Hen. VI.* ii. 5: "blowing of his nails;" *J. C.* v. 3: "saving of thy life;" *A. Y. L.* ii. 7: "hearing of a song;" etc.

*In this sad knot.* Folded thus.

*Still-vex'd Bermoothes.* The ever-disturbed Bermudas. "The epithet here applied to the Bermudas," says Henley, "will be best understood by those who have seen the chafing of the sea over the rugged rocks by which they are surrounded, and which render access to them so dangerous." On *still*=ever, see *Mer.* p. 128.

*Who, with a charm.* See above on *Who t' advance,* etc.

*For the rest of the fleet.* This use of *for*=*as for, as regards,* is common in S. See Gr. 149.

*Flote.* Flood, wave. Probably the same as *float,* and not the French *flot,* as most editors make it.

*Two glasses.* Two turns of the hour-glass, two hours.

*Since thou dost give me pains.* Dost give me hard work to do.

*Let me remember thee.* Remind thee. Gr. 291. Cf. *W. T.* iii. 2: "I'll not remember you of my own lord," etc. It is sometimes used in a similar sense (=mention) without an object; as in 2 *Hen. IV.* v. 2:—

> "Our coronation done, we will accite,
> As I before remember'd, all our state."

Cf. below, "The ditty does remember (mention, or commemorate) my drown'd father." The passive form *to be remembered* is sometimes=to call to mind, to recollect; as, "If you be remember'd" (*M. for M.* ii. 1, and *T. of S.* iv. 3), "I am remember'd" (*A. Y. L.* iii. 5), "Be you remember'd" (*T. A.* iv. 3), etc.

*Is not yet perform'd me.* The *me* is the "indirect object" of the verb. Gr. 220. Cf. just below, "To do me business."

*To bate me.* Cf. *A. W.* ii. 3: "I will not bate thee a scruple." See also *Mer.* p. 153.

*To tread the ooze.* The bottom (not the margin) of the sea. Cf. *Hen. V.* 1. 2: "the ooze and bottom of the sea;" and below, iii. 3: "my son i' th' ooze is bedded."

*Hast thou forgot.* On the form of the participle, see Gr. 343, and cf. *Mer.* p. 141, note on *Not undertook.*

*Argier.* The old name for Algiers. It was not obsolete even in Dryden's day. See his *Limberham*, iii. 1: "you Argier's man."

*For one thing she did.* But what it was the poet nowhere tells us. It may have been mentioned (as Boswell thinks) in the novel on which the play was probably founded.

*This blue-eyed hag.* Staunton suggests "blear-eyed," but no change is necessary.

*Wast then her servant.* The folio has *was*, and (as Walker suggests) that may be what S. wrote. So below the folio has "stroked'st and made much of me."

*And for thou wast.* And because thou wast. See Gr. 151, and *Mer.* p. 134, note on *For he is a Christian.*

*Hests.* Commands. Sometimes printed "'hests," but it is not a contraction of *behests.* It is used again in iii. 1 ("I have broke your hest"), and in iv. 1 ("spongy April at thy hest betrims"); and it is used by Wiclif, Chaucer, Spenser, etc. The mistake in printing *'hest* is like that of *'bate* (see *Mer.* p. 153), *yond'* (see C. p. 369), *'light* (=alight), etc.

*Into a cloven pine.* We sometimes find *into* for *in* "with verbs of rest implying motion" (cf. *Rich. III.* v. 5: "Is all my armour laid into my tent?"), as we often find *in* with verbs of motion (cf. *M. of V.* v. 1: "creep in our ears;" *Ham.* v. 1: "leaping in her grave," etc.). "Fall in love" is still a familiar idiom. A few lines below we have "put heaviness in me."

*Caliban her son.* Farmer says, "The *metathesis* in *Caliban* from *Canibal* is evident."

*Correspondent to command.* That is, obedient to command. See Gr. p. 12 (viii).

*And do my spriting gently.* Do my work as a spirit meekly, or with good will (as opposed to "moody" above). Some editors print "spiriting," but the folio has "spryting." "Spirit" is often virtually a monosyllable. Gr. 463.

*Go make thyself*, etc. The folio reads thus:

> "Goe make thy selfe like a Nymph o' th' Sea,
> Be subject to no sight but thine, and mine: inuisible
> To euery eye-ball else," etc.

This is well enough with a slight change in arrangement, as in the text; but Steevens omits the *thine* as "ridiculous," and prints the lines as follows:

> "Go make thyself like to a nymph o' the sea;
> Be subject to no sight but mine; invisible," etc.

This reading is adopted by D., but not by W. or H.

*We cannot miss him.* Cannot do without him; the only instance of this sense in S., or elsewhere, so far as I know.

*Come, thou tortoise! when?* Cf. *J. C.* ii. 1: "When, Lucius, when?" *Rich. II.* i. 2: "When, Harry, when?" *T. of S.* iv. 1: "Why, when, I say?" etc. *What* and *why* were similarly used as impatient exclamations. See *Mer.* p. 141, note on *What, Jessica!*

*Fine apparition! My quaint Ariel.* So below, "fine spirit," "fine Ariel," and "delicate Ariel." On *quaint*, see *Mer.* p. 141.

*Wicked dew.* Baneful, poisonous. Cf. Chaucer, *Rom. of the Rose:* "a fruict of savour wicke."

*Urchins.* Mischievous elves. Cf. *M. W.* iv. 4: "urchins, ouphes (elves), and fairies." They were probably called so because they somctimes took the form of urchins, or hedgehogs. Cf. below (ii. 2) Caliban's account of Prospero's spirits:

> "Then like hedgehogs, which
> Lie tumbling in my barefoot way, and mount
> Their pricks at my footfall."

*That vast of night.* That void, waste, or empty stretch. In *Ham.* i. 2, the quarto of 1603 has "In the dead vast and middle of the night," but the other old editions have "wast." In modern editions we find "vast," "waste," and "waist" (=middle).

*Whiles you do keep from me.* On *whiles*, see *Mer.* p. 133, and Gr. 137.

*Abhorred slave*, etc. The folio gives this speech to *Miranda*, but this is obviously an error of the type.

*Which any print*, etc. On *which*, "used interchangeably with *who* and *what*," see Gr. 265.

*Confined into this rock.* See above on *Into a cloven pine.*

*My profit on't.* For *on't*, see *Mer.* p. 143, or Gr. 182.

*The red plague.* The leprosy. See *Levit.* xiii. 42, 43. Jephson explains it as the erysipelas.

*Rid you.* Destroy you. Cf. *Rich. II.* v. 4: "will rid his foe," and 3 *Hen. VI.* v. 5: "you have rid this sweet young prince."

*Learning me your language.* Cf. *Cymb.* i. 5: "Hast thou not learned me how To make perfumes?" In old English the word meant to *teach* as well as to learn. See Rich. and Gr. 291.

*Thour't best.* Cf. *J. C.* iii. 3: "Ay, and truly, you were best." For other examples of this old idiom, see Gr. 230.

*Old cramps.* Abundant cramps. On this intensive or augmentative use of *old* in colloquial language, see *Mer.* p. 161.

*Aches.* The noun *ache* used to be pronounced *aitch*, but the verb *ake* (as it is often printed). Baret, in his *Alvearie* (1580), says: "*Ake* is the Verbe of the substantive *ach*, *ch* being turned into *k*." That the noun was pronounced like the name of the letter *h* is evident from a pun in *Much Ado.* iii. 4:

> "*Beatrice.* . . . By my troth, I am exceeding ill! Heigh-ho!
> *Margaret.* For a hawk, a horse, or a husband?
> *Beatrice.* For the letter that begins them all, H."

There is a similar joke in *The World Runs upon Wheels*, by John Taylor, the Water-poet: "Every cart-horse doth know the letter *G* very understandingly; and *H* hath he in his bones." Boswell quotes an instance of this pronunciation from Swift, and Dyce one from Blackmore, A.D. 1705. When John Kemble first played Prospero in London, he pronounced *aches* in this passage as a dissyllable, which gave rise to a great dispute on the subject among critics. During this contest Mr. Kemble was laid up with sickness, and Mr. Cooke took his place in the play. Everybody listened eagerly for his pronunciation of *aches*, but he *left the whole line out;* whereupon the following appeared in the papers as "*Cooke's Soliloquy:*"

> "*Aitches* or *akes*, shall I speak both or either?
> If *akes* I violate my Shakespeare's measure—
> If *aitches* I shall give King Johnny pleasure;
> I've hit upon't—by Jove, I'll utter neither!"

*That beasts shall tremble.* *So* that; a common ellipsis. Gr. 283.

*No, pray thee.* This omission of *I* before *pray thee, beseech thee*, etc., is very common. See Gr. 401.

*Setebos.* S. probably got this name from the account of Magellan's voyages in Robert Eden's *History of Travaile* (A.D. 1577), where it is said of the Patagonians that "they roared lyke bulles, and cryed uppon their great devill, Setebos, to help them." Malone says that Setebos is also mentioned in Hakluyt's *Voyages*, 1598.

*Curtsied.* So spelled in the folio. *Curtsy* and *courtesy* are two forms of the same word, both found in the folio. In a single speech in *J. C.* iii. 1, we have "courtesies" and "curtsies."

*And kiss'd The wild waves whist.* That is, kissed the wild waves into silence; "a delicate touch of poetry that is quite lost as the passage is usually printed, the line *The wild waves whist* being made parenthetical, and that, too, without any authority from the original" (H). *Whist* is the participle of the old verb *whist*, which is found both transitive and intransitive. Lord Surrey translates the first line of Book II. of the *Æneid:* "They whisted all, with fixed face attent." Cf. Spenser, *F. Q.* vii. 7, 59: "So was the Titanesse put downe and whist." Milton (*Hymn on Nativ.*) has the same rhyme as here:

> "The winds with wonder whist
> Smoothly the waters kiss'd."

*Foot it featly.* Dexterously, neatly. D. quotes Lodge's *Glaucus and Scilla* (1589): "Footing it featlie on the grassie ground." Cf. *W. T.* iv. 3: "she dances featly." We have the adjective (used adverbially) below, ii. 1: "much feater than before;" and in *Cymb.* i. 1, the verb (=fashioned, moulded): "a glass that feated them." On the *it*, see Gr. 226.

*Where should this music be?* As Abbott remarks (Gr. 325), "*should* was used in direct questions about the past where *shall* was used about the *future*."

*Weeping again.* That is, again and again. Gr. 27. Cf. *M. of V.* iii. 2: "For wooing here until I sweat again."

*With it's sweet air.* In the folio *its* occurs but once (*M. for M.* i. 2), while *it's* is found nine times. *It* as a genitive (or "possessive") is found fourteen times, in seven of which it precedes *own*. This *it* is "an early provincial form of the old genitive." In our version of the Bible *its* is found only in *Levit.* xxv. 5, where the original edition has "of it own accord." See Gr. 228, *Bible Word-Book*, pp. 272–275, and C. pp. 160–171.

*Full fathom five.* The folio has "fadom," which Halliwell and White prefer to retain.

*Of his bones are coral made.* S. may have written *are* to avoid the harshness of "bones is," but the inaccuracy is probably to be classed with those given by Abbott (Gr. 412) under "confusion of proximity." Some make *coral* a plural.

*Those are pearls*, etc. In *Rich. III.* iv. 4, we have *tears* "transform'd to orient pearl."

*Ding, dong, bell.* Cf. the *Song* in *M. of V.* iii. 2.

*Nor no sound that the earth owes.* On the double negative, see *Mer.* p. 131, and Gr. 406. *Owes*=owns, as often in S. See Gr. 290.

*The fringed curtains of thine eyes.* Cf. *Per.* iii. 2: "her eyelids Begin to part their fringes of bright gold."

*What thou seest yond.* *Yond* is the A. S. *geond*=*illuc*. *Yond*, meaning outrageous, furious (as in Spenser, *F. Q.* iii. 7, 26: "As Florimell fled from that Monster yond"), is probably the same word; though Kitchin (Clarendon Press edition of Spenser's *F. Q. Bk. II.* p. 296) gives a different etymology.

*A brave form.* On *brave*=fine, gallant, etc., see *Mer.* p. 154.

*And but he's something stained.* On *but*=except, etc., see Gr. 120.

*Most sure, the goddess.* Cf. the *O dea certe* of Virgil (*Æn.* i. 328).

*Vouchsafe my prayer may know . . . and that you will.* Here we have "*that* omitted and then inserted," Gr. 285. Cf. *Rich II.* v. 1: "Think I am dead, and that even here," etc.

*If you be maid.* The fourth folio has *made* (that is, created, or mortal), which some modern editors adopt.

*A single thing.* A feeble thing. Cf. *Macb.* i. 3: "shakes so my single state of man."

*His brave son.* This son is not one of the *dramatis personæ*, nor is he elsewhere mentioned in the play.

*More braver.* See above on *More better.*

*Control thee.* "Confute thee, unanswerably contradict thee." (Johnson.)

*Changed eyes.* Exchanged looks of love.

*Done yourself some wrong.* Misrepresented yourself. Cf. *M. W.* iii. 3: "This is not well, Master Ford, this wrongs you."

*Pity move my father.* An example of "the subjunctive used optatively." See Gr. 364.

*O, if a virgin, and your affection not gone forth.* On the ellipsis, see Gr. 387.

*In either's powers.* See Gr. 12. In *Sonnet* 93 we have "In many's looks."

*That thou attend me.* "The subjunctive after verbs of command and entreaty is especially common." Gr. 369. For the omission of the preposition, cf. *M. of V.* v. 1: "When neither is attended," and see Gr. 200.

*Ow'st not.* Ownest not. Cf. above, "that the earth owes."

*On't.* See *Mer.* p. 143, and Gr. 182.

*There's nothing ill can dwell.* On the omission of the relative, see Gr. 244.

*I'll manacle thy neck and feet together.* The cut illustrates this mode of punishment better than any description could do.

*Gentle and not fearful.* Of gentle blood, and therefore no coward. Smollett (in *Humphrey Clinker*) says: "To this day a Scotch woman in the situation of the young lady in *The Tempest* would express herself nearly in the same terms—Don't provoke him; for, being *gentle*, that is, *high spirited*, he won't tamely bear an insult."

*My foot my tutor!* "Shall my heel teach my head? Shall that which I tread upon give me law?" (V.) Walker (*Crit. Ex.* iii. p. 3) proposes *fool*, which D. adopts.

*Come from thy ward.* Leave thy posture of defence. *Ward* was a technical term in fencing. Cf. 1 *Hen. IV.* ii. 4: "Thou knowest my old ward; here I lay, and thus I bore my point."

*Beseech you, father!* See above on *No, pray thee.*

*There is no more such shapes.* The reading of the folio, changed by many editors (including D., W., and H.) to "there are." But "there is" is often found preceding a plural subject. Gr. 335. Cf. *Cymb.* iii. 1: "There is no more such Cæsars" (where D., W., and H. all have "is"); *Id.* iv. 2: "There is no more such masters" (D. and W. have "is," and the former defends it in a note, but H. has "are"), etc. So in questions we find, "Is there not charms?" (*Oth.* i. 1); "Is all things well?" (2 *Hen. VI.* iii. 2); "Is there not wars?" (2 *Hen. IV.* i. 2), etc.

*All corners else o' th' earth.* All other parts. Cf. *M. of V.* ii. 7: "the four corners of the earth" (so in *Isa.* xi. 12), *Cymb.* iii. 4: "all corners of the world," etc. In *K. John* (v. 7) we find "the *three* corners of the world."

## ACT II.

SCENE I.—*Our hint of woe.* The cause of our sorrow. See on *It is a hint*, i. 2.

*The masters of some merchant.* This is the reading of the folio, and is somewhat doubtful, though *masters* may mean *owners*, or possibly *officers*. Steevens suggested "mistress" (the old spelling of which is sometimes "maistres"), and V. thinks it "not improbable" that this was S.'s word. D. and others read "master." The Camb. editors conjecture "master's" (*sc.* wife). The first *merchant* means a merchant vessel, or *merchantman*, as we say even now. Malone quotes Dryden (*Parallel of Poetry and Painting*): "Thus as convoy-ships either accompany or should accompany their merchants."

*The visitor.* An allusion to priestly visitants of the sick or afflicted. Cf. *Matt.* xxv. 36.

*One: —tell.* There may be a play on *one* and *on* (that is, *go* on), the two words (see Nares on *One*) being pronounced, and sometimes written, alike. *Tell*=count. We still say "all told," "wealth untold," "to tell one's beads," etc., and a *teller* is one who *counts* (money, votes, etc.).

*Dolour.* Cf. the same play upon words in *M. for M.* i. 2, and *Lear*, ii. 4. Steevens quotes also *The Tragedy of Hoffman*, 1637:

> "And his reward be thirteen hundred dollars,
> For he hath driven dolour from our heart."

*Which, of he or Adrian.* This is the reading of the folio. Cf. *M. N. D.* iii. 2:

> "Now follow, if thou dar'st, to try whose right,
> Of thine or mine, is most in Helena."

Walker (*Crit. Ex.* iii. p. 353) quotes from Sidney's *Arcadia*: "Who should be the former [that is, the first to fight] against Phalantus, of the black or the ill-apparelled knight." Gr. 206, 409.

*The cockrel.* The young cock; that is, Adrian.

*Ha, ha, ha!* The folio gives this speech to Sebastian, and *So, you're paid* to Antonio, and perhaps there is no need of change. On the whole, however, I prefer to follow W., who simply transposes the prefixes of the speeches on the ground that "Antonio won the wager, and was paid by having the laugh against Sebastian." Theo. gave both speeches to Sebastian, and is followed by D. and the Camb. editors. Capell and H. merely change "you're" to "you've." K. and C. retain the folio reading.

*Temperance.* Temperature. Antonio takes up the word as a female name, and it was so used by the Puritans.

*Lush.* Juicy, succulent, luxuriant. Not elsewhere used by S., though some read in *M. N. D.* ii. 1, "Quite overcanopied with lush woodbine" where the folio has "luscious." *Lusty*=vigorous.

*An eye of green.* A tinge of green. Boyle says, "Red, with an eye of blue, makes a purple."

*Freshness and glosses.* The folio has "freshnesse and glosses." *Freshness* may be plural, like *princess* in i. 2 ("Than other princess can"). See note on that passage. D. reads "gloss."

*A paragon to their queen.* For their queen. Cf. *J. C.* iii. 1: "I know that we shall have him well to friend;" *Rich. II.* iv. 1: "I have a king here to my flatterer;" also *Matt.* iii. 9; *Luke*, iii. 8, etc. Below (iii. 2) we find "that hath to instrument this lower world."

*Widow Dido.* This was the title of a popular song of that day. See Percy's *Reliques*, or Prof. Child's *English and Scottish Ballads*, vii. p. 207.

*Study of that.* Study about that; wonder what you mean by it. See Gr. 174.

*The miraculous harp.* An allusion to the myth of Amphion, who raised the walls of Thebes by the power of his music.

*In my rate.* In my estimation, or reckoning. Cf. above (i. 2), "all popular rate."

*Whose enmity he flung aside*, etc. Cf. *J. C.* i. 2:

> "The torrent roared; and we did buffet it
> With lusty sinews; throwing it aside,
> And stemming it with hearts of controversy."

*His wave-worn basis.* *His* for *its*. See Gr. 228.

*I not doubt.* This omission of the auxiliary *do* in negative sentences is quite common. See below (v. 1), "whereof the ewe not bites," "I not know," and "I not doubt;" and 2 *Hen. IV.* iv. 1: "It not belongs to you." See also Gr. 305.

*Who hath cause to wet the grief on't.* Which hath cause to weep. The antecedent of *who* is *eye*. Cf. 2 *Hen. IV.* iv. 3: "The heart Who great and puff'd up." See Gr. 264.

*Which end o' th' beam she'd bow.* The folio has "should bow," which is probably a misprint for "sh'ould bow."

*The dear'st o' th' loss.* "Throughout S., and all the poets of his and a much later day, we find this epithet (*dearest*) applied to that person or thing which, for or against us, excites the liveliest interest. . . . It may be said to be equivalent generally to *very*, and to import the excess, the utmost, the *superlative* of that to which it is applied." (Caldecott.) Cf. "dearest enemy" (1 *Hen. IV.* iii. 2), "dearest foe" (*Ham.* i. 2), "dearest need" (*Rich. III.* v. 2), "dearest groans" (*A. W.* iv. 5), etc. See also C. p. 292, and D. (*Glossary*). Cf. below (v. 1), "dear loss."

*Had I plantation.* There is a play on the word *plantation*. Gonzalo uses it in the sense of *colony* (cf. Bacon, *Ess.* xxxiii., *Of Plantations*), but Antonio takes it in the sense of *planting*.

*I' th' commonwealth*, etc. This passage is evidently copied from Florio's translation of Montaigne's *Essays*, published in 1603, and therefore aids (see *Introduction*, page 8) in fixing the date of the play. W. gives the quotation from Florio, as follows: "It is a nation, would I answere *Plato*, that hath *no kinde of traffike*, no *knowledge of Letters*, no intelligence of numbers, *no name of magistrate*, nor of politike superioritie; no *use of service, of riches, or of povertie; no contracts, no successions, no dividences, no occupation, but idle*; no respect of kinred, but common; no apparell, but naturall; no manuring of lands; *no use of wine, corn, or mettle.* The very words that import lying, falsehood, *treason*, dissimulation, covetousness, envie, detraction, and pardon were never heard amongst them."*

* The original runs thus: "C'est une nation, diroy ie a Platon, en laquelle il n'y a

*Of it own kind.* See above (i. 2) on *With it's sweet air.*

*Foison.* Plenty. The word is French (*fuison* in Old French), the Latin *fusio*, from *fundere.*

*T' excel th' golden age.* As to excel. Cf. *M. of V.* iii. 3: "So fond to come abroad;" and see Gr. 281.

*Sensible and nimble.* Sensitive and excitable. See *Mer.* p. 145. Cf. *Ham.* ii. 2: "the clown shall make those laugh whose lungs are tickled o' th' sere" (that is, tickled with a dry cough).

*An it had not fallen flat-long.* On *an*, see *Mer.* p. 131, and Gr. 101. *Flat-long*, that is, as if struck with the side of the sword instead of its edge. *Flatling* is used in the same sense; as in Spenser, *F. Q.* v. 5, 18: "Tho with her sword on him she flatling strooke."

*A bat-fowling.* On *a*, see Gr. 140. *Bat-fowling* was a method of fowling by night, in which the birds were started from their nests and stupefied by a sudden blaze of light. Markham, in his *Hunger's Preuention, or the Whole Arte of Fowling*, says, "I thinke meete to proceed to Battefowling, which is likewise a nighty taking of all sorts of great and small Birdes which rest not on the earth, but on Shrubbes, tal Bushes, Hathorne trees, and other trees, and may fitly and most conueniently be used in all woody, rough, and bushy countries, but not in the champaine." He goes on to describe the process. D. (*Glossary*) quotes the passage in full.

*Adventure my discretion.* That is, *venture* or risk my [character for] discretion. Cf. *T. G. of V.* iii. 1: "So bold Leander would adventure it;" *Cymb.* i. 7: "that I have adventur'd to try," etc.

*Omit the heavy offer of it.* Neglect the offer of its heaviness. *Omit* often means to pass over, lay aside, or neglect; as above (i. 2): "Whose influence, if I court not, but omit;" *Oth.* ii. 1: "do omit their mortal natures;" *M. for M.* iv. 3: "What if we do omit This reprobate till he were well inclin'd?" etc.

*What thou shouldst be.* On *should=ought*, see Gr. 323.

*The occasion speaks thee.* "The opportunity which now occurs shows what you are intended for; that is, to be a king" (Jephson).

*If heed me.* That is, if you intend to heed me. Such ellipses in conditional sentences are common in S. See Gr. 383–393. Cf. above (i. 2), "O, if a virgin," etc.

*Trebles thee o'er.* That is, over again. See Gr. 58 a, and cf. *M. of V.* iii. 2: "I would be trebled twenty times myself."

*I am standing water.* Jephson interprets this, "I am stagnant, slow of understanding and action." It seems to me rather to mean, I am passive, ready to listen to you and to be influenced by you. He already guesses what Antonio means, and cherishes the purpose while he mocks it.

Steevens quotes the following from a critic in the *Edinburgh Magazine* for Nov. 1786: "Sebastian introduces the simile of water. It is taken up by Antonio, who says he will teach his stagnant water to flow. 'It has

aulcune espece de trafique, nulle cognoissance de lettres, nulle science de nombres, nul nom de magistrat ni de superiorité politique, nul usage de service, de richesse ou de pauvreté, nuls contracts, nulles successions, nuls partages, nulles occupations qu'oysifves, nul respect de parenté que commun, nuls vestements, nulle agriculture, nul metal, nul usage de vin ou de bled; les paroles mesmes qui signifient le mensonge, la trahison, la dissimulation, l'avarice, l'envie, la detraction, le pardon, inouyes."

already learned to ebb,' says Sebastian. To which Antonio replies, 'O, if you but knew how much even that metaphor, which you use in jest, encourages to the design which I hint at; how, in stripping the words of their common meaning, and using them figuratively, you adapt them to your own situation!'"

*This lord of weak remembrance.* "This lord who, being now in his dotage, has outlived his faculty of remembering; and who, once laid in the ground, shall be as little remembered himself as he can now remember other things" (Johnson).

*He's a spirit of persuasion.* Monk Mason thought that "he's" is for "he has," not "he is," and quotes 1 *Hen. IV.* i. 2: "Well, mayst thou have the spirit of persuasion," etc. Steevens regarded the words "professes to persuade" as a marginal gloss or paraphrase, which by some mistake became incorporated with the text, and D. appears to favor this view. Johnson could "draw no sense" from "this entangled sentence," but there seems to be no special difficulty in it. The parenthesis is clearly marked in the folio, thus:

> "(For hee's a Spirit of perswasion, onely
> Professes to perswade) the King his sonne's aliue," etc.

*But doubts discovery there.* But doubts whether there is any thing to be discovered there. The folio has "doubt," which the Philadelphia editors think "may be retained;" "but doubt" being considered equal to "without doubting," or the "can not" being mentally carried on: "[can not] but doubt discovery there."

*Beyond man's life.* An obvious and intentional hyperbole. Hunter (*New Illustrations*, i. p. 166) thinks that *Man's Life* is probably the translation of the name of some African city, and finds an ancient city, named *Zoa*, not far from Tunis.

*The man i' th' moon.* This is one of the oldest of popular superstitions. According to one version, the man who gathered sticks on the Sabbath (*Numb.* xv. 32 foll.) was imprisoned in the moon; but another tradition made this lunar personage to be Cain. In the *Testament of Cresseid* (written by Henryson, but sometimes ascribed to Chaucer) we find the following in a description of the moon:

> "Hir gyse was gray, and full of spottis blak,
> And on hir breist ane churle paintit ful evin,
> Beirand ane bunche of thornis on his bak,
> Quhilk for his thift micht clim na nar the hevin."
> [Laing's ed., 1865.]

It will be recollected that the man in the moon is one of the characters in the clowns' play in *M. N. D.* See iii. 1, and v. 1.

*Can take no note.* Can receive no information. Cf. Bacon, *Ess.* xlix.: "that if Intelligence of the Matter could not otherwise have beene had but by him, Advantage bee not taken of the Note, but the Partie left to his other Meanes."

*She from whom.* That is, in coming from whom. The folio has "She that from whom." The emendation was made by Rowe, and is adopted by D., H., W., and others.

*In yours and my discharge.* *Is* in yours, etc.; that is, "depends on what you and I are to perform" (Steevens). "*Act* and *prologue* being technical terms of the stage, *discharge* also is so to be understood, as in *M. N. D.* i. 2 : 'I will discharge it in either your straw-coloured beard,' etc." (Phila. ed.)

*Measure us back.* *Us* refers to that which is supposed to "cry out," or "every cubit."

*There be that can rule Naples.* See *Mer.* p. 134 (note on *There be land-rats*), and Gr. 300.

*Could make a chough of as deep chat.* Could train a chough to talk as wisely. Cf. *A. W.* iv. 1 : "chough's language, gabble enough, and good enough." Yarrel (*History of British Birds*) observes that in the description of Dover Cliff ("The crows and choughs that wing the midway air," *Lear*, iv. 6), "possibly S. meant jackdaws, for in the *M. N. D.* he speaks of 'russet-pated' (gray-headed) choughs, which term is applicable to the jackdaw, but not to the real chough."

*How does your content tender*, etc. How does your favorable judgment regard. For *tender*=regard, value, cf. *Hen. V.* ii. 2 : "But we our kingdom's safety must so tender;" *A. Y. L.* v. 2 : "By my life, I do; which I tender dearly," etc.

*Much feater.* More neatly or trimly. See on *Foot it featly*, i. 2, and Gr. 1.

*If it were a kibe*, etc. If it were a sore heel, it would make me exchange my boot for a slipper. Cf. *Ham.* v. 1 : "the toe of the peasant comes so near the heel of the courtier, he galls his kibe."

*That's dead.* Farmer suggested that these words are a gloss, or marginal note, that has somehow found its way into the text.

*This ancient morsel.* That is, Gonzalo.

*Should not upbraid.* On *should*, see Gr. 322.

*Suggestion.* Temptation, "hint of villainy" (Johnson). Cf. below (iv. 1), "the strong'st suggestion Our worser Genius can." The verb is likewise used in the sense of tempt, incite, seduce; as in *A. W.* iv. 5 : "I give thee not this to suggest thee from thy master;" *T. G. of V.* iii. 1 : "Knowing that tender youth is soon suggested," etc.

*I'll come by Naples.* Cf. *M. of V.* i. 1. "But how I caught it, found it, or came by it," and see Gr. 145.

*When I rear my hand.* Cf. *J. C.* iii. 1 : "Casca, you are the first that rears your hand."

*To fall it.* See *Mer.* p. 135, and Gr. 291. Cf. below (v. 1), "fall fellowly drops."

*To keep thee living.* The folio has "keepe them liuing."

*Why are you drawn?* Why are your swords drawn? See Gr. 374. Cf. *R. and J.* i. 1 : "What, art thou drawn among these heartless hinds?" and, again, "What, drawn, and talk of peace!" See also *M. N. D.* iii. 2, and *Hen. V.* ii. 1.

*I shak'd you.* S. generally uses *shook*, both as past tense and participle, but he has *shak'd* in five instances, in three of which it is the participle. In 1 *Hen. IV.* iii. 1, we find *shak'd* once and *shook* three times in a single scene. See *Mer.* p. 141 (note on *Not undertook*).

*That's verily.* The reading of the folio, changed by most of the editors to "That's verity." See Gr. 78.

SCENE II.—*By inch-meal.* Inch by inch. We still have *piece-meal* (not used by S.), but *inch-meal, limb-meal* (*Cymb.* ii. 4: "tear her limb-meal"), *drop-meal*, and other compounds of the kind are obsolete. *Meal* in these words is the A. S. *mæl* (time, portion), not *melu, melo* (meal, flour).

*Urchin-shows.* Elfin apparitions. See above (i. 2) on *Urchins.*

*Mow.* Make faces. Cf. below (iv. 1), "with mop and mow;" and the stage direction in iii. 3, "*with mocks and mows.*" Not from *mouth*, as some have made it, but (see Diez, Scheler, and Wb.) from the French *moue* (pouting, wry face).

*And after bite me.* Cf. *J. C.* i. 2: "And after scandal them."

*Mount their pricks.* Raise their prickles. Cf. *Henry VIII.* i. 1: "The fire that mounts the liquor till't run o'er;" and *Id.* i. 2: "mounting his eyes."

*And to torment me.* For the *and*, see Gr. 95 and 96.

*Yond.* See on *What thou seest yond*, i. 2.

*Bombard.* Also spelled *bumbard;* a large flagon, or "black-jack," made of leather. Cf. 1 *Hen. IV.* ii. 4: "that huge bombard of sack." *Foul* (which Upton wished to change to *full*) probably means black with age and decayed—ready to fall to pieces.

*Poor-john.* A cant name for salted *hake*, a coarse and cheap kind of fish. Cf. *R. and J.* i. 1: "'Tis well thou art not fish; if thou hadst, thou hadst been poor John." So in Massinger's *Renegado*, i. 1:

> "To feed upon poor-john, when I see pheasants
> And partridges on the table."

In B. and F.'s *Scornful Lady* (ii. 3), "pitch and poor-john" are mentioned as the foul odors of Thames Street, London.

*A doit.* See *Mer.* p. 136.

*A dead Indian.* Cf. just below, "savages and men of Ind." There may be an allusion to the Indians brought home by Sir Martin Frobisher in 1576.

*Gaberdine.* See *Mer.* p. 135.

*I will here shroud.* Take shelter. Both noun and verb were thus used. Cf. *A. and C.* iii. 13: "Put yourself under his shroud" (his protection). See also Milton, *Comus*, 147: "Run to your shrouds;" and 316: "Or shroud within these limits;" Spenser, *F. Q.* i. 1, 8: "therein shrouded from the tempest dread," etc.

*As proper a man.* See *Mer.* p. 132 (note on *A proper man's picture*).

*At nostrils.* In the folio this is printed "at' nostrils," and may be a misprint for "at's nostrils." We find, however, "at mouth" (*J. C.* i. 2), "at heart" (*A. Y. L.* i. 2), "on knees" (*T. and C.* v. 3.), "on nose" and "on side" (*A. Y. L.* ii. 7), and the like. See Gr. 90.

*Afore.* This form was common in old English, and so was *to-fore*, which we find in *T. A.* iii. 2: "O, would thou wert as thou to-fore hast been!"

*I will not take too much for him.* That is, I will take all I can get.

*Will give language to you, cat.* Alluding to the proverb, "Good liquor will make a cat speak." A few lines below, there is an allusion to the proverb, "He hath need of a long spoon, that eats with the devil."

*Siege.* Stool, excrement. It is used in the same sense by Ben Jonson and Sir Thomas Browne. Besides its ordinary meaning, it has also in S.

the sense of *seat* (*M. for M.* iv. 2: "the siege of justice"), and of *rank*, or *place* (*Ham.* iv. 7: "the unworthiest siege;" *Oth.* i. 2: "men of royal siege").

*Moon-calf.* A monstrosity, supposed to be occasioned by lunar influence. In Holland's *Pliny* (vii. 15) we find, "a moone-calfe, that is to say, a lump of flesh without shape, without life."

*An if.* See Gr. 101–103.

*Hast any more of this?* For the ellipsis of the subject, see Gr. 401, 402.

*Thy dog and thy bush.* See above on *The man i' th' moon*, and cf. *M. N. D.* iii. 1, etc. The "bush" was the bundle of sticks connected with the narrative in *Numb.* xv.

*Afeard.* See *Mer.* p. 144.

*Well drawn, monster.* A good draught, monster.

*Crabs.* Crab-apples. "Roasted crabs" are mentioned in *L. L. L.* v. 2 (Song), and *M. N. D.* ii. 2. Cf. *Lear*, i. 5: "as like this as a crab is like an apple."

*Scamels.* This is the reading of the folio, but the word is found nowhere else. Some have thought it a diminutive of *scam*, a name by which the limpet is said to be known in some parts of England; others read "sea-mells" or "sea-malls" (the latter form is actually found as the name of a bird in Holme's *Acad. of Armory*, 1688); and others "stannels" or "staniels." Of these emendations the last is perhaps the most plausible. Montagu (*Ornithological Dict.*) says that the "Kestrel, *Stannel*, or Windhover . . . is one of our most common species [of hawks], especially *in the more rocky situations and high cliffs on our coasts, where they breed.*" The bird is also mentioned by S. in *T. N.* ii. 5: "And with what wing the staniel checks at it!" At least, no one doubts that this is the correct reading, though the old editions print "stallion."

*Trenchering.* The reading of the folio, changed to *trencher* by Theo., D., H., and most of the editors; but, as W. remarks, "surely they must have forgotten that Caliban was drunk, and after singing 'firing' and 'requiring' would naturally sing 'trenchering.' There is a drunken swing in the original line, which is entirely lost in the precise, curtailed rhythm of—

> 'Nor scrape *trencher*, nor wash dish.'"

---

## ACT III.

Scene I.—*There be some sports are painful.* See *Mer.* p. 134, and Gr. 300 and 244. *Painful*=requiring pains, or laborious. Cf. *L. L. L.* ii. 1: "painful study;" *T. of S.* v. 2: "painful labour both by sea and land." Fuller (*Holy War*, v. 29) speaks of Joseph as "a painful carpenter," and in his *Holy State* (ii. 6) he says, "O the holiness of their living, and painfulness of their preaching!"

*Delight in them sets off.* *Delight* is the subject of *sets off*, which is here equivalent to *offsets.* Cf. *Macb.* ii. 3: "The labour we delight in physics pain."

*The mistress which.* See Gr. 265.

*Most busy, least when I do it.* "This is the great *crux* of the play. Few passages in S. have been the subject of more conjecture, and to none has conjecture been applied with less happy results." The first folio reads, "Most busie lest, when I doe it;" the other three folios, "Most busie least, when I do it." Pope reads, "Least busie when I do it." Theo. gave "Most busie-less when I do it;" and Dr. Johnson puts "busiless" into his Dict., citing this passage to justify it. Neither Worc. nor Wb. recognizes the word. The editors from Theo. (1733) down to the *Var.* of 1821 adopted "busiless," and of recent editors D. and H. (the latter without comment) have followed them. The difficulty of the passage is well shown by the vacillation of the best modern critics. D. in his 2d ed. (1864) says that "busiless' is "far more satisfactory, on the whole, than any of the numerous emendations that have been proposed;" while in his 1st ed. (1857) he doubts "if so odd a compound ever occurred to anybody but the critic himself." K. in 1839 followed Theo., but in 1864 he adopts the reading of the later folios, defending it thus: "The opposition of *most* and *least* renders the line somewhat obscure; but if we omit *most*, reading 'Busy least when I do it,' the sense is clear enough. It is not less clear with *most*, so punctuated." W. in his *Shakespeare's Scholar* (1854) accepts "busy-less," and considers "busiest" to be "graceless and inappropriate;" but in his edition of S. (1857) he reads "busiest," adding this note: "The present text is the happy conjecture of Holt White. *Busiest* of course refers to *thoughts*. Ferdinand's 'sweet thoughts' of Miranda were busiest when he was labouring to win her."

Of the other attempts at emendation the following are worthy of mention: Collier's MS. corrector's "Most busy-blest when I do it;" Staunton's "Most busy felt when I do it;" Spedding's "Most busiest when idlest;" the Camb. editors, "Most busied left when idlest;" and Keightley's "Most busy, lest when I do it—."

I have preferred, on the whole, to follow Verplanck and retain the reading of the folios ("lest" and "least" may be regarded as identical), with the slight change in punctuation. The passage may then be explained as follows: "In these reflections I forget my labours, which are even refreshed with the sweetness of the thoughts, and I am really most busy in mind, while I am least busy with my task—occupied with my thoughts, idlest with my hands." I take this paraphrase from the Phila. ed., where the passage, with the various readings and criticisms, is very fully and ably discussed.

On the transposition in "least when," cf. above (i. 2), "Curtsied when you have," etc. For the various forms of transposition in S., see Gr. 419–427.

*But yours it is against.* Cf. *A. and C.* ii. 4: "Hasten your generals after;" *A. W.* iii. 4: "That barefoot plod I the cold ground upon," etc. Gr. 203.

*Visitation.* Visit; its ordinary meaning in S. He does not use *visit* as a noun. Cf. *M. of V.* iv. 1: "in loving visitation was with me," etc.

*Hest.* See on this word above (i. 2). It occurs three times in this play, but nowhere else, unless we adopt the reading of the 1st Quarto in 1 *Hen. IV.* ii. 3: "On some great sudden hest;" where all the other old editions have "haste," or "hast," which is another spelling of the same word.

*Admir'd Miranda!* Ferdinand refers to the Latin origin of the name, from the gerundive of *mirari*, to admire.

*The top of admiration.* Cf. *M. for M.* ii. 2: "the top of judgment;" 2 *Hen. VI.* i. 2: "top of honor;" *Cor.* i. 9: "top of praises," etc.

*Several.* Separate. Cf. v. 1: "strange and several noises." So in Milton, *Com.* 25: "commits to several government;" *Hymn on Nativ.* 234: "Each fetter'd ghost slips to his several grave," etc.

*Owed.* Owned. See on the same word, i. 2.

*To like of.* Cf. *Much Ado*, v. 4: "if you like of me;" *L. L. L.* i. 1: "But like of each thing that in season grows;" *Rich. III.* iv. 4: "Richard likes of it," etc. See also Gr. 177.

*Than to suffer.* Pope changed this to "Than I would suffer;" but the insertion of *to* with a verb after its omission with a preceding one (especially an auxiliary) is not uncommon in S. See Gr. 350.

*If hollowly.* Cf. *M. for M.* ii. 3:

> "And try your penitence, if it be sound,
> Or hollowly put on."

*What else i' th' world.* Whatever else there is, anything else. Cf. 3 *Hen. VI.* iii. 1: "With promise of his sister and what else." See Gr. 255.

*Your maid.* Your maid-servant.

*Your fellow.* Your companion. The word was applied to both sexes. Cf. *Judges* xi. 37 and *Psa.* xlv. 14 (*Prayer-Book* version). *Companion* was formerly used contemptuously, as *fellow* still is. Cf. *J. C.* iv. 3: "Companion, hence!" and 2 *Hen. VI.* iv. 10: "Why, rude companion, whatso-e'er thou be." It is found in this sense even in so late a work as Smollett's *Roderick Random* (1748): "Scurvy companion! Saucy tarpaulin! Rude, impertinent fellow!"

*Whether you will or no.* This use of *no*, though common in old writers, is condemned by modern grammarians. See F. 523, note x.

*A thousand thousand.* That is, farewells.

*Who are surpris'd with all.* On *who* (=for they), see Gr. 263. *With all*, the reading of the folio, was changed by Theo. to *withal*, and D. follows him. W. and H. read *with all*.

*I'll to my book.* For the ellipsis, see Gr. 405.

SCENE II.—*There's but five.* See on *There is no more such shapes*, i. 2.

*Standard.* Standard-bearer, or ensign. The quibbles on this word, and on *lie*, just below, are obvious enough.

*Debosh'd.* This is the old spelling of *debauched*, and is found in the folio in the four instances in which S. uses the word (*A. W.* ii. 3 and v. 3, *Lear*, i. 4, and here).

*That a monster should be such a natural!* A quibble on *natural* as opposed to *monstrous* and as=*fool*.

*But this thing dare not.* That is, would not dare. Gr. 361.

*Pied ninny.* Alluding to the motley dress of the professional jester, or fool, as the name *patch* (see *Mer.* p. 142) perhaps does.

*Quick freshes.* Springs of fresh water. *Quick* (=living) is applied to water flowing from a spring, as "living" is in the Bible and elsewhere. S. does not elsewhere use *fresh* as a noun, but it is found in other old writers.

*Wezand.* Throat, windpipe. The word is omitted by Mrs. Clarke in her *Concordance.*

*A sot.* A fool (the French *sot*). This is its only meaning in S. Cf. *C. of E.* ii. 2: "Thou snail, thou slug, thou sot!" *Lear*, iv. 2: "he called me sot, And told me I had turn'd the wrong side out," etc.

*And that most deeply to consider.* For the omission of the relative, see Gr. 244.

*Troll the catch.* Sing the tune. A *catch* is a *round*, in which the parts are taken up (or *caught* up) in succession. *Troll*, as a noun, means the same as *catch* (see Wb.); and *to troll* was to sing as in a troll, or catch.

*While-ere.* A while ago. See Gr. 137.

*The picture of Nobody.* Probably an allusion to a ludicrous figure (head, arms, and legs, without a trunk, or *body*) printed on the old popular ballad of *The Well-spoken Nobody.* (Halliwell.)

*Take 't as thou list.* "Take what shape pleases thee."

*Will hum*, etc. See on *I'd divide*, i. 2. The Phila. ed. says that this use of *will* to "express a custom" is not mentioned by grammarians and lexicographers. It had been mentioned by F. (§ 522, 21) at least ten years before the criticism was made, and this very passage from the *Temp.* is quoted as an illustration of the idiom.

*In dreaming.* For other examples of in = *while*, or *during*, see Gr. 161.

*That when I waked.* *So* that. See Gr. 283.

Scene III.—*By 'r Lakin.* By our Ladykin, or the Virgin Mary. The diminutive, as often, expresses endearment = our *dear* Lady.

*My old bones aches.* The folio has *akes.* See on *Aches*, i. 2; and for the form of the verb, on *What cares these roarers*, i. 1.

*Forth-rights and meanders.* Straight paths and winding ones. Cf. *T. and C.* iii. 3: "Or hedge aside from the direct forth-right." There is an allusion to the artificial "mazes" of the olden time.

*Attach'd with weariness.* Seized with weariness. *Attach* is etymologically the same as *attack*, and is often found in that sense. Cf. Spenser, *F. Q.* iii. 8, 33:

> "Like as a fearefull partridge, that is fledd
> From the sharpe hauke which her attached neare."

*Will we take throughly.* See *Mer.* p. 144 (note on *Throughfares*) and p. 158.

*A living drollery.* A *drollery* was a puppet-show. Cf. 2 *Hen. IV.* ii. 1: "a pretty slight drollery."

*One tree the phœnix' throne*, etc. In Holland's translation of Pliny's *Nat. Hist.* (xiii. 4) we read: "I myself verily have heard straunge things of this kind of tree; and namely in regard of the bird *Phœnix*, which is supposed to have taken that name of this date-tree [called in Greek φοινιξ]; for it was assured unto me that the said bird died with that tree, and revived of itselfe as the tree sprung again." Lyly, in his *Thoughts*, says: "As there is but one phœnix in the world, so is there but one tree in Arabia wherein she buildeth." Florio, in his *Ital. Dict.*, defines "Rasin" as "a tree in Arabia, whereof there is but one found, and upon it the phœnix sits." See also the opening lines of the poem of *The Phœnix and the Turtle*, in the *Passionate Pilgrim.*

*Certes.* Certainly. The word was nearly obsolete in S.'s day. He uses it only five times. It is a favorite archaism with Spenser.

*I cannot too much muse.* That is, wonder at it. Cf. *Macb.* iii. 4: "Do not muse at me;" 2 *Hen. VI.* iii. 1: "I muse my lord of Gloster is not come," etc. We find the word also as a noun = wonderment; as in Spenser, *F. Q.* i. 12, 29: "he sate long time astonished, As in great muse."

*Praise in departing.* A proverbial expression. Praise given too soon may have to be retracted.

*Dew-lapp'd like bulls.* Doubtless a reference to the victims of *goître*, so common in mountainous districts, especially in some parts of Switzerland.

*Whose heads stood in their breasts.* Cf. *Oth.* i. 3: "men whose heads do grow beneath their shoulders." Pliny (*Nat. Hist.* v. 8) tells of men that have no heads, but mouths and eyes in their breasts; and Hakluyt, in his *Voyages* (1598), describes "a nation of people whose heads appear not above their shoulders." Bucknill (*Medical Knowledge of Shakespeare*) suggests that the poet "may only refer to the effect produced by forward curvature of the spine, in which the head appears to be set below the shoulders."

*Each putter-out of five for one.* Thus in the folio. Theo. suggested "on five for one," which W. adopts. Malone (followed by D.) reads "of one for five." Collier, K., the Camb. editors, and H. retain the reading of the folio, which may be explained as "*at the rate of* five for one." The allusion is to "a kind of inverted life insurance" which was in vogue in S.'s day. A traveller before leaving home *put out* a sum of money, on condition of receiving two, three, or five times the amount upon his return. If he did not return, of course the deposit was forfeited. Cf. Ben Jonson's *Every Man out of his Humour*, ii. 3: "I am determined to put forth some five thousand pounds, to be paid me, five for one, upon the return of myself, my wife, and my dog, from the Turk's court in Constantinople. If all or either of us miscarry in the journey, 'tis gone: if we be successful, why, there will be twenty-five thousand pounds to entertain time withal."

*Whom Destiny . . . hath caused to belch up you.* On the supplementary pronoun, see Gr. 249. *Up you* may be an accidental transposition, as W. regards it; but see Gr. 240.

*Hath to instrument.* Hath *for* or *as* instrument. See on *A paragon to their queen*, ii. 1.

*Such like.* See Gr. 278.

*Their proper selves.* Their own selves. Cf. *Cymb.* iv. 2: "With my proper hand," etc.

*The elements Of whom.* Cf. above (ii. 1), "your eye Who hath cause;" and see Gr. 264.

*Bemock'd-at.* Cf. "hoped-for" (3 *Hen. VI.* v. 4), "sued-for" (*Cor.* ii. 3), "unthought-on" (*W. T.* iv. 4), "unthought-of" (1 *Hen. IV.* iii. 2), etc. See Gr. 431.

*Still-closing.* Cf. above (i. 2), "still-vexed Bermoothes," and see *Mer.* p. 128.

*Dowle.* A fibre of down. The word is probably (see Wb.) a corruption of *down*. In 2 *Hen. IV.* iv. 4, the folio has "There lyes a dowlney feather," and in the next line "that light and weightlesse dowlne."

*Are like invulnerable.* Alike invulnerable. Prof. Allen (Phila. ed.) suggests printing it "'like" (cf. "'las!" for "alas!"), as he finds no example of *like=alike.*

*Requit.* Cf. "Have quit it," i. 2, and see Gr. 342.

*Than any death Can be at once.* Than any death-at-once can be. For many similar examples of transposed "adjectival phrases," see Gr. 419 *a.*

*Which here . . . else falls.* On the number of the verb, see Gr. 247.

*Is nothing.* This ellipsis of *there* is not uncommon. See Gr. 404.

*Clear life.* Pure, blameless. Cf. *Lear*, iv. 6: "the clearest gods." So in *The Two Noble Kinsmen*, i. 1: "for the sake Of clear virginity."

*With good life And observation strange.* Johnson says: "*With good life* may mean 'with exact presentation of their several characters,' *with observation strange* 'of their particular and distinct parts.' So we say, 'he acted to the *life*.'" Or, *good life* may mean "good spirit," and *observation strange* "wonderfully exact observance" [of my orders, or of the requirements of the part]. *Observation* is elsewhere=observance; as in *M. N. D.* iv. 1: "For now our observation is performed." On *strange*, cf. "strangely stood the test," iv. 1.

*Whom they suppose is drown'd.* Other examples of this confusion of two constructions are *K. John*, iv. 2: "Of Arthur, whom they say is killed to-night;" and *Cor.* iv. 2: "The nobility . . . whom we see have sided." Cf. *Matt.* xvi. 13.

*Mine lov'd darling.* See Gr. 238.

*Bass.* Utter in a deep tone. W. prints "base," but there can be no good reason for following the spelling of the folio.

*But one fiend.* Let but one fiend come.

*This ecstasy.* This madness. In S. *ecstasy* "stands for every species of alienation of mind, whether temporary or permanent, proceeding from joy, sorrow, wonder, or any other exciting cause." (Nares.)

---

## ACT IV.

SCENE I.—*A thread of mine own life.* The folio reads "a third," which, as D. remarks, "is rather an old spelling than a mistake: in early books we occasionally find *third* for *thrid*, i. e. *thread*." V. retains "third," but K., Sr., St., W., H., and others read "thread."

*Who once again.* For *who=whom*, see *Mer.* pp. 131, 143, and Gr. 274.

*Virgin-knot.* Alluding to the zone or girdle which was worn by maidens in classical times, and which the husband untied at the wedding. Hence *solvere zonam*=to marry. Cf. *Per.* iv. 3: "Untied I still my virgin-knot will keep."

*Aspersion.* Literally, sprinkling. There is perhaps an allusion to the old ceremony of sprinkling the marriage-bed with holy water in token of blessing.

*Opportune.* The accent is on the penult. Cf. *W. T.* iv. 4: "And most opportune to our need I have." See Gr. 490.

*Our worser genius can.* S. uses *worser* fifteen times. *Can;* i. e. "can suggest," as some explain it; or *can* may be = to have power, to be able. See *Mer.* p. 133 (note on *May you stead me?*), and Gr. 307.

*The edge of that day's celebration*, etc. "The keen enjoyment of the celebration of our wedding-day." (Jephson.)

*Fairly spoke.* The *-n* or *-en* of the participle is often dropped by the Elizabethan writers. See Gr. 244.

*What would my potent master?* See *Mer.* p. 135 (note on *How much you would*).

*The rabble.* That is, "thy meaner fellows."

*Some vanity.* Some illusion. Cf. the old romance of *Emare*:

> "The emperour sayde on hygh,
> Sertes, thys ys a fayry,
> Or ellys a vanyte."

*Presently?* Immediately. See *Mer.* p. 131.

*Mop and mow.* The two words have the same meaning (see on *Mow*, ii. 2), and are often thus conjoined in writers of that day. Cf. B. and F., *Pilgrim*, iv. 2:

> "What mops and mowes it makes! heigh, how it frisketh!
> Is 't not a fairy? or some small hob-goblin?"

*White-cold.* The folio has "white cold," but it is probably a compound adjective, like "sudden-bold" (*L. L. L.* ii. 1), "fertile-fresh" (*M. Wives*, v. 5), "active-valiant" and "valiant-young" (1 *Hen. IV.* v. 1), etc. See Gr. 2.

*My liver.* The liver was anciently supposed to be the seat of love. Cf. *Much Ado*, iv. 1: "if ever love had interest in his liver."

*A corollary.* A surplus. See Wb.

*Pertly.* Briskly, promptly.

*Stover.* Fodder for cattle. It has the same origin as the law-term *estovers* (see Wb.). In some parts of England, according to Jephson, it means hay made of clover. *Thatch'd* probably means "covered, strewn," and not, as it has been explained, "having shelters thatched with straw."

*Pioned and lilied.* The folio has "pioned, and twilled," which some editors have retained, explaining it as "dug and ridged." Steevens says that Spenser has *pioning* = digging. Rowe changed "twilled" into "tuliped," and Capell into "tilled." Others have changed "pioned" to "pionied" and "peonied;" but Dr. Johnson gives "piony" as another form for "peony," and the spelling of the folio may as well stand. The peony may not suit our modern taste as a flower for "chaste crowns," but old writers are quoted who call it "the mayden piony" and "virgin peonie." It has been objected that peonies and lilies do not bloom in April, but Boswell quotes Bacon's Essay *Of Gardens*: "In *Aprill* follow, The Double white Violet; The Wall-Flower; The Stock-Gilly-Flower; The Couslip; Flower-De-lices, and Lillies of all Natures; Rose-mary Flowers; The Tulippa; The Double Piony;" etc.

*Broom groves.* Groves in which broom (*Spartium scoparium*) abounds; though Steevens asserts that the broom itself sometimes grows "high enough to conceal the tallest cattle as they pass through it, and in places where it is cultivated still higher." Hanmer changed "broom" to "brown."

*Lass-lorn.* Forsaken by his lass, or lady.

*Pole-clipt.* Not "clipped so as to be trained to a pole" (as Jephson explains it), but with the poles *clipt*, or embraced, by the vines. S. uses *clip* (including *inclip* once) fourteen times* in this obsolete sense, and only three times in its ordinary sense.—*Vineyard* is probably here a trisyllable. See Gr. 487.

*Watery arch and messenger.* Iris was the goddess of the rainbow, and also the messenger of Juno.

*Bids thee leave these, and . . . to come.* See on *Than to suffer*, iii. 1.

*Her peacocks.* The chariot of Juno was drawn by peacocks, as that of Venus was by doves (see "Dove-drawn," a few lines below).

*Amain.* Literally, *with main* (which we still use in "might and main"), that is, with strength or force, vigorously.

*Saffron wings.* Cf. Virgil, *Æn.* iv. 700: "Iris croceis . . . pennis."

*Bosky.* Wooded. Cf. Milton, *Com.* 313: "every bosky bourn."

*Estate.* Grant, or settle as a possession. Cf. *M. N. D.* i. 1: "all my right of her I do estate unto Demetrius." See also *A. Y. L.* v. 2.

*The means that dusky Dis*, etc. The means by which Pluto carried off Proserpina. See Ovid, *Met.* v. 363 foll. For the epithet, cf. the "atri . . . Ditis" of Virgil (*Æn.* vi. 127), etc.

*Blind boy's.* Cf. *M. N. D.* i. 1: "therefore is wing'd Cupid painted blind," etc.

*Paphos.* A city in Cyprus, one of the favorite seats of Venus.

*Thought they to have done.* Cf. below, "I thought to have told thee," and see Gr. 360.

*Mars's hot minion.* Mars's ardent favorite. Venus was the wife of Vulcan, but loved Mars. *Minion*, originally equivalent to "darling" (Fr. *mignon*), came at length to mean "an unworthy object on whom an excessive fondness is bestowed." In Sylvester's *Du Bartas* (1605) we find "God's disciple and his dearest minion." So in Stirling's *Domes-day:* "Immortall minions in their Maker's sight."

*Has broke.* See on *Fairly spoke*, above.

*I know her by her gait.* Cf. Virgil, *Æn.* i. 46: "divum incedo regina."

*Marriage, blessing.* So pointed in folio. Most of the editors print "marriage-blessing," which may be what S. wrote.

*Earth's increase, foison plenty.* The reading of the folio. The second folio has "and foison," which is adopted by many editors. See Gr. 484.

All the early editions give the whole Song to Juno. Theo. made the correction.

*Spring come to you*, etc. Cf. *Amos*, ix. 13.

*Their confines.* Their abodes in air, earth, water, etc. Cf. *Ham.* i. 1:

> "Whether in sea or fire, in earth or air,
> The extravagant and erring spirit hies
> To his confine."

*So rare a wonder'd father and a wise.* Cf. *K. John*, iv. 2: "So new a fashion'd robe;" *C. of E.* iii. 2: "So fair an offer'd chain," etc. See Gr. 422. The Phila. ed. states that some copies of the folio read "wise," and others "wife." The change must have been made while the book was

* The Phila. ed. says "thirteen," but one instance in *The Passionate Pilgrim* is omitted.

printing, but which is the corrected reading can not now be determined. All the other folios have "wise." Rowe reads "wife," and is followed by Pope, Theo., Capell, Johnson, and the *Var.* eds., without note or comment. D. gave "wise" in his 1st ed., but changes it to "wife" in the 2d. K., on the other hand, has "wife" in the 1st ed. and "wise" in the 2d. Sr. has "wife;" St., "so rare a wonder, and a father wise;" the Camb. editors, "wife;" W. and H. "wise."

*Winding brooks.* The folio has "windring," and it is doubtful whether we should read "wand'ring" or "winding."

*Sedg'd crowns.* Cf. Milton's description of the river-god Camus (*Lyc.* 104): "his bonnet sedge." Walker (*Crit. Ex.*) suggests "sedge" here.

*Crisp channels.* Rippled or ruffled by the wind. Cf. Milton, *P. L.* iv. 237: "the crisped brooks;" and *Com.* 984: "the crisped shades and bowers." Some explain it here as "curling or winding channels." Either interpretation is better than Jephson's: "because of the crisply curled verdure on their banks."

*Avoid!* Depart, begone! Cf. *A. and C.* v. 2: "Avoid, and leave him;" *W. T.* i. 2: "Let us avoid," etc. Cf. 1 *Sam.* xviii. 11.

*Distemper'd.* Disturbed, excited. Cf. *R. and J.* ii. 3: "a distemper'd head;" *K. John*, iv. 3: "distemper'd lords," etc. See Gr. 439.

*Leave not a rack.* The folio has "racke." *Rack*, as applied to the clouds, is not the same word as *wracke*=wreck (see Wb.), but old writers often spelled them both "rack" or "racke." The critics are not agreed which is the word here. The best plea for *rack* (=vapor) may be found in the Phila. ed.; the best for *wrack* (or *wreck*) in D.'s 2d ed., vol. i., p. 253. The weight of argument seems to me slightly in favor of the latter, which W. adopts. H. takes the other view. It may be remarked that we still have *rack*=*wreck* in "rack and ruin."

*Made on.* See *Mer.* p. 143 (note on *Glad on't*), and Gr. 181, 182.

*Presented Ceres.* Represented, personated. Cf. *M. Wives*, iv. 6: "present the fairy queen." In *M. N. D.* (iii. 1 and v. 1) it occurs several times in this sense. See also Milton, *Il Pens.* 99: "Presenting Thebes, or Pelops' line."

*Unback'd colts.* Cf. the description of the effect of music on "unhandled colts," *M. of V.* v. 1.

*Bring it hither.* For the redundant *it*, see Gr. 243, 417.

*Stale.* Decoy, bait. Cf. B. and F., *Hum. Lieut.* iii. 2: "Stales to catch kites;" Sidney, *Arcadia:* "But rather one bird caught served as a stale to bring in more;" Spenser, *F. Q.* ii. 1. 4: "he craftie stales did lay," etc.

*Hang them on this line.* The folio has "on them." *Line* is the old name for the *lime* or linden tree, used below (v. 1) in "line-grove." Hunter (*New Illust.*, vol. i., p. 179) understands the tree to be meant here; but, as D. has suggested, Stephano's joke, "Now, jerkin, you are like to lose your hair," has no point unless we assume the "line" to be a *hair-line.* "Buy a hair-line" is one of the cries in an old wood-cut of 1611, illustrating the trades and callings of that day; and in Lyly's *Midas*, a barber's apprentice facetiously says, "All my mistres' lynes that she dryes her cloathes on, are made only of Mustachio stuffe" (i. e. of the cuttings of moustaches).

*Play'd the Jack.* The Jack-o'-lantern, or Will-of-the-Wisp.

*Good my lord.* My good lord. Cf. *J. C.* ii. 1: "Dear my lord;" *R. and J.* iii. 5: "Sweet my mother;" *T. and C.* v. 2: "O poor our sex!" See Gr. 13.

*I, thy Caliban.* See *Mer.* p. 152 (note on *You and I*), and Gr. 209.

*O King Stephano! O peer!* An allusion to the old song, "Take thy old cloak about thee," one stanza of which (quoted in *Oth.* ii. 3) begins, "King Stephen was a worthy peer," etc.

*A frippery.* A shop for second-hand clothes.

*To dote.* For the construction, see Gr. 356.

*Let's alone.* The reading of the folio. Theo. read "Let's along," which D. adopts. Malone proposed "Let it (or Let't) alone," and is followed by Collier, V., and H. W. retains the old reading, explaining it thus: "Let us do the murder alone, without the Fool's aid." In iii. 2, Caliban says to Stephano:

> "If thy greatness will,
> Revenge it on him, for I know thou dar'st;
> But this thing [Trinculo] dare not."

*Jerkin.* A kind of doublet.

*To lose your hair.* A quibbling allusion to the loss of hair from fever (or other disease) in crossing the line, or equator.

*Pass of pate.* Sally of wit. *Pass* (=thrust) is a term in fencing.

*Lime.* That is, bird-lime.

*Barnacles.* Probably not the shell-fish, but the geese into which these were supposed to be transformed. Marston (*Malcontent*, iii. 1) says:

> "like your Scotch barnacle, now a block,
> Instantly a worm, and presently a great goose."

For a full account of this old superstition, and an explanation of its origin, see Max Müller's *Lect. on the Science of Language, Second Series*, pp. 552–571 (Amer. ed.).

*Villanous low.* See Gr. 1.

*Lies at my mercy*, etc. See on *What cares these roarers*, i. 1. D., W., and H. read "Lie," but there is no reason for changing the old construction. *Lies* is found plural in S. at least five times, in three of which the rhyme forbids any change.

---

## ACT V.

SCENE I.—*His carriage.* His load, burden. Cf. *K. John*, v. 7: "For many carriages he hath despatch'd." See also *Judges*, xviii. 21; 1 *Sam.* xvii. 22; *Isa.* x. 28; *Acts*, xxi. 15, etc.

*Line-grove.* Changed by most editors to "lime-grove;" but see on *Hang them on this line*, iv. 1.

*Weather-fends.* Defends from the weather. See Gr. 432.

*Till your release.* Till you release them. *Your* is a "subjective genitive."

*Him that you term'd.* On *him* = he, see Gr. 208.

*His tears runs.* The reading of the folio. Most editors have "run." See Gr. 333.

*That relish all as sharply Passion.* That "feel everything with the same quick sensibility," or that are fully as sensitive to suffering.

*Ye elves*, etc. Some expressions in this speech may have been suggested by Medea's speech in Ovid's *Metamorphoses* (book vii.), which S. had probably read in Golding's translation:

> "Ye ayres and windes, ye *elves of hills, of brookes, of woodes* alone,
> *Of standing lakes*, and of the night, approche ye everych one,
> *Through help of whom* (the crooked bankes much wondering at the thing)
> I have compelled streames to run clean backward to their spring.
> By charmes I make the calm seas rough, and make the rough seas playne,
> And cover all the skie with clouds, and chase them thence again;
> By charmes *I raise and lay the windes*, and burst the viper's jaw,
> And from the bowels of the earth both stones and trees do draw;
> Whole woodes and forrests I remove, *I make the mountains shake*,
> And even the earth itself to groan and fearfully to quake.
> *I call up dead men from their graves*, and thee, O lightsome moone,
> I darken oft, though beaten brass abate thy peril soone:
> Our sorcerie dimmes the morning faire, and *darks the sun at noone*.
> The flaming breath of fierie bulles ye quenched for my sake,
> And caused their unwieldy neckes the bended yoke to take.
> Among the earth-bred brothers you a *mortal warre did set*,
> And brought asleep the dragon fell, whose eyes were never shet."

*Green sour ringlets.* "Fairy rings," or circles on the grass supposed to be made by the elves in their nightly dances. Dr. Grey (*Notes on S.*) says they "are higher, sowrer, and of a deeper green than the grass which grows round them." They were long a mystery even to scientific men. Priestley (1767) ascribed them to the effects of lightning; Pennant (1776) and others, to the burrowing of moles, by which the soil was loosened and thus made more productive; Wollaston (1807), to the spreading of a kind of *agaricum*, or fungus, which enriches the ground by its decay. This last explanation is now known to be the correct one.

*Mushrooms.* The folio has the old form, "mushrumps."

*Weak masters.* This is commonly explained, "weak if left to yourselves," though powerful auxiliaries (as we say that "fire is a good servant, but a bad master"); but Jephson thinks that "*masters* is only used ironically, as a term of slight contempt." Of the two interpretations I prefer the latter; but the "irony" is affectionate rather than contemptuous.

*Azur'd.* See Gr. 294.

*Their senses that.* The senses of those whom. See Gr. 218.

*A solemn air*, etc. May this solemn air, which is the best comforter, etc.

*Boil'd.* Cf. *M. N. D.* v. 1: "seething brains;" and *W. T.* iii. 3: "these boiled brains of nineteen and two-and-twenty."

*Sociable to the show of thine.* Sympathizing with what appears in thine.

*Fall fellowly drops.* Cf. ii. 1: "to fall it on Gonzalo." Gr. 291. On *fellowly*, see Gr. 447.

*Apace.* At (or with) a quick pace, rapidly; a compound, like *amain* (with main, or strength).

*I will pay thy graces Home.* I will repay thy favors to the utmost, or thoroughly. Cf. *M. for M.* iv. 3: "Accuse him home and home." *Cymb.* iii. 5: "satisfy me home;" and v. 2: "that confirms it home." We still say "charge home" (*Cor.* i. 4) and "strike home" (*T. A.* ii. 1 and 3).

*You, brother mine.* On the use of *you* here, followed by *thee* in "I do forgive thee," etc., see Gr. 232.

*Remorse and nature.* Pity and natural affection. See *Mer.* p. 156, and cf. *C. of E.* i. 1: "was wrought by nature, not by vile offence."

*Reasonable shore.* Shore of reason.

*Discase me.* Undress myself. Cf. *W. T.* iv. 3: "therefore discase thee." This reflexive use of the personal pronoun is common in S. See Gr. 223.

*Sometime.* Formerly. See *Mer.* p. 130.

*I do fly After summer.* Cf. *M. N. D.* iv. 1: "Trip we after the night's shade;" and Milton, *Hymn of Nativ.* 236: "Fly after the night-steeds," etc. Theo. changed "summer" to "sunset," and other critics have made sad work of the Song by attempts to improve the pointing of the folio, which is essentially as I have given it, following V., W., D., and H. The meaning is well brought out by V.: "At night, 'when owls do cry,' Ariel couches 'in a cowslip's bell;' and he uses 'the bat's back' as his pleasant vehicle to pursue summer in its progress round the world, and thus live merrily under continual blossoms." It has been objected that bats do not "fly after summer," but become torpid in winter; but, even if the poet had known this zoological fact, he might none the less have made Ariel use the creature for his purposes. The "tricksy spirit" was not limited by natural laws.

*Being awake.* For the construction, see Gr. 376.

*Or ere.* See note on the same phrase, i. 2.

*Inhabits.* Another example of the old plural. See Gr. 333, 336.

*Trifle to abuse me.* Phantom to deceive me. Cf. *Ham.* ii. 2: "Abuses me to damn me." We have the same expression in B. and F. (*Bonduca*, v. 2): "In love too with a trifle to abuse me."

*I not know.* See on *I not doubt*, ii. 1, and cf. "the ewe not bites," etc.

*Since I saw thee.* We should now say "have seen thee." See Gr. 347.

*An if this be at all.* If indeed there be any reality in it. "And if" in the folio. See Gr. 103, 105.

*Taste some subtilties of the isle.* "This is a phrase adopted from ancient cookery and confectionery. When a dish was so contrived as to appear unlike what it really was, they called it a *subtilty.* Dragons, castles, trees, etc., made out of sugar, had the like denomination." (Steevens.)

*Pluck.* Bring down. Cf. *A. W.* iii. 2: "pluck his indignation on thy head."

*Justify you traitors.* Prove you traitors. Cf. *A. W.* iv. 3: "*Second Lord.* How is this justified? *First Lord.* The stronger part of it by her own letters."

*I am woe for't.* I am sorry for it. Cf. *A. and C.* iv. 14: "Woe, woe are we, sir." In *Cymb.* v. 5, we find "I am sorrow for thee." See Gr. 230.

*Of whose soft grace.* By whose kind favor.

*As late.* As *it is* recent; but some explain it, "*and* as recent."

*Supportable.* Accent on the first syllable. Cf. "*détestáble*" (*K. John*, iii. 4; *T. of A.* iv. 1) and "*délectáble*" (*Rich. II.* ii. 3). Gr. 492. (Abbott himself is inclined to put it under 497. Steevens reads "portable," a word used by S. in this sense in *Lear*, iii. 6, and *Macb.* iv. 3.

*Have I means.* For the transposition, see Gr. 425.

*That they were living.* "The subjunctive used optatively." Gr. 364.

*Myself were mudded*, etc. For "myself" as subject, see *Mer.* p. 137 (note on *Yourself*). Cf. iii. 3: "my son i' th' ooze is bedded; . . . And with him there lie mudded."

*Do so much admire.* Do so much wonder.

*Which was thrust forth of Milan.* See Gr. 266 and 166.

*To content ye.* On *ye*, see Gr. 236. *Content* (cf. the French *contenter*) often = "please" or "delight" in S. Cf. *Ham.* ii. 2: "it doth much content me to hear him."

"*Here Prospero discouers Ferdinand and Miranda, playing at Chesse.*" Such is the stage direction in the folio. It is the only allusion to chess in S., unless there be a punning one in *T. of S.* i. 1, where Katherine says, "I pray you, sir, is it your will To make a *stale* of me amongst these *mates?*" Steevens thinks that the introduction of the game here was suggested by the romance of *Huon de Bordeaux*, where "King Ivoryn caused his daughter to play at the chesse with Huon," etc. But, as Prof. Allen suggests in an interesting *Excursus* in the Phila. ed., even if S. *did* take a hint from that old romance, it was probably because he was aware that there was a *special* appropriateness in representing a prince of *Naples* as a chess-player, since Naples, in the poet's day, "was the centre of chess-playing," and probably famed as such throughout Europe.

*Play me false.* Cheat me. Cf. Gr. 220.

*If this prove*, etc. H. says: "The sense of this passage is not altogether clear. The word *not* seems wanting after *prove*; unless *if* have by some means got substituted for *but.* Alonso has lost his son once, and if this which he now sees prove *not* a mere vision, he will have to lose him again." I can see no difficulty in the passage. If this be a mere vision, his son is *not* restored to him, and he must *again* give him up as lost.

*I am hers.* That is, her father.

*Chalk'd forth the way.* We should say "chalk'd out the way." Cf. *Hen. VIII.* i. 1:

"Chalks successors their way."

*No man was his own.* Was master of himself, or in his senses.

*Still embrace.* Ever embrace. See *Mer.* p. 128.

*Here is more of us.* See on *There is no more such shapes*, i. 2.

*Safely found Our King and company.* That is, found them safe. Cf. just below, "freshly beheld Our royal, good, and gallant ship." S. often uses adverbs as "predicate adjectives," a fact not mentioned by Abbott, though he refers to the use of adverbs for adjectives after *is* (78). Cf. above (iii. 1), "look wearily" for "look weary." So in *M. Wives*, ii. 1: "looks so merrily;" *A. Y. L.* i. 2: "he looks successfully," etc. But elsewhere we have "looks pale," "looks sad," "look stern," "look fair," etc. We find also the adjective for the adverb, as in 1 *Hen. VI.* i. 2: "Meantime look gracious on thy prostrate thrall," etc. The two constructions are often confounded by good writers even in our day.

*Gave out split.* Gave up as gone to pieces. In 2 *Hen. VI.* iv. 8, "given out these arms" means given them up.

*Yare.* See on *Yarely*, i. 1.

*Tricksy.* Steevens (followed by Dyce) explains the word as "clever, adroit;" Jephson as "pretty or engaging;" others as "cunning, sportive," etc. Rich. (*Dict.*) defines it "trickish, artful, dexterous, adroit, active, smart," and cites Warner, *Albion's Eng.* vi. 31:

"There was a tricksie girle, I wot,
Albeit clad in grey,
As peart as bird, as straite as boult,
As fresh as flower in May."

Florio (*Ital. Dict.*) defines *Pargoletta* as "quaint, pretty, nimble, trixie, tender, small."

*Dead of sleep.* The folio reading. Malone read "on sleep" (Cf. *Acts* xiii. 36), but *on* and *of* were often used interchangeably, as indeed they still are by illiterate people. See Gr. 180, 182. Abbott himself puts this under 168 (*of*="as a consequence of").

*But even now.* Just now. See Gr. 38.

*Several.* Separate, distinct; as in iii. 1, and iii. 3.

*Capering to eye her.* Jumping for joy at the sight of her.

*On a trice.* We say "in a trice," as S. does elsewhere. In *Lear*, i. 1. we have "in this trice of time."

*Moping.* The folio has "moaping," and some editors print "mopping" (=grimacing). The Phila. ed. explains it rightly: "Depressed and moping, because suddenly interrupted in the midst of their rejoicing, separated from their companions, and 'enforced' to go, whither they knew not, by some irresistible supernatural power."

*Conduct of.* Conductor of. Cf. *Rich. II.* iv. 1: "I will be his conduct;" *R. and J.* v. 3: "Come, bitter conduct, come, unsavoury guide!"

## EPILOGUE.

It is well known that the Prologues and Epilogues of the English Drama are generally written by other persons than the authors of the plays, and White with good reason thinks that this Epilogue, though printed in the folio, bears internal evidence of being no exception to the rule. The thoughts are "poor and commonplace," and the rhythm is "miserable and eminently un-Shakespearian." It is apparently from the same pen as the Epilogue to *Henry VIII.*—"possibly Ben Jonson's, whose verses they much resemble." The Epilogue to the *Second Part of Henry IV.* is another that is evidently not Shakespeare's; and it is a significant fact that, in the folio, these three Epilogues "are plainly pointed out as separate performances." "For in these plays the characters are all sent off the stage by the direction *Exeunt*, and the Epilogue is set forth as something apart from the play, being, in one case, separated from it by a single rule, in another by double rules, and in the third being printed on a page by itself, while in the other plays the *Exeunt* or *Exit* is not directed until after the Epilogue, which is included within the single border-rule of the page, no separation of any kind being made." A comparison of the various Epilogues shows that "this arrangement has no reference to the personage by whom the Epilogue is to be spoken;" and, as no other explanation of it can be given, it is probable that the editors of the folio meant thus to indicate that the Epilogues are not Shakespeare's.

*With the help of your good hands.* "By your applause, by clapping hands" (Johnson). Noise was supposed to dissolve a spell. Cf. above (iv. 1): "hush! be mute; Or else our spell is marr'd."

*Unless I be reliev'd by prayer.* "This alludes to the old stories told of the despair of necromancers in their last moments, and of the efficacy of the prayers of their friends for them" (Warburton). Jephson thinks it may be an allusion to "the custom, prevalent in S.'s time, of concluding the play by a prayer, offered up kneeling, for the sovereign."

*Mercy itself.* The divine Mercy.

*Frees all faults.* Frees *from* all faults. See Gr. 200.

CALIBAN [Act II., Scene 2].

Caliban [Act II., Scene 2].

THE END.

# SHAKESPEARE.

## WITH NOTES BY WM. J. ROLFE, A.M.

THE MERCHANT OF VENICE.
THE TEMPEST.
JULIUS CÆSAR.
HAMLET.
HENRY THE FIFTH.
MACBETH.
TWELFTH NIGHT.
AS YOU LIKE IT.
HENRY THE EIGHTH.
RICHARD THE SECOND.
A MIDSUMMER-NIGHT'S DREAM.
MUCH ADO ABOUT NOTHING.
ROMEO AND JULIET.
OTHELLO.
WINTER'S TALE. (*In Press.*)

ILLUSTRATED. 16MO, CLOTH, 70 CENTS PER VOLUME; PAPER, 50 CENTS PER VOLUME.

In the preparation of this edition of the English Classics it has been the aim to adapt them for school and home reading, in essentially the same way as Greek and Latin Classics are edited for educational purposes. The chief requisites of such a work are a pure text (expurgated, if necessary), and the notes needed for its thorough explanation and illustration.

Each of Shakespeare's plays is complete in one volume, and is preceded by an Introduction containing the "History of the Play," the "Sources of the Plot," and "Critical Comments on the Play."

*From* HORACE HOWARD FURNESS, Ph.D., LL.D., *Editor of the "New Variorum Shakespeare."*

In my opinion Mr. Rolfe's series of Shakespeare's Plays is thoroughly admirable. No one can examine these volumes and fail to be impressed with the conscientious accuracy and scholarly completeness with which they are edited. The educational purposes for which the notes are written Mr. Rolfe never loses sight of, but like "a well-experienced archer hits the mark his eye doth level at."

*From* F. J. FURNIVALL, *Director of the New Shakspere Society, London.*

The merit I see in Mr. Rolfe's school editions of Shakspere's Plays over those most widely used in England is that Mr. Rolfe edits the plays as works of a poet, and not only as productions in Tudor English. Some editors think that all they have to do with a play is to state its source and explain its hard words and allusions; they treat it as they would a charter or a catalogue of household furniture, and then rest satisfied. But Mr. Rolfe, while clearing up all verbal difficulties as carefully as any Dryasdust, always adds the choicest extracts he can find, on the spirit and special "note" of each play, and on the leading characteristics of its chief personages. He does *not* leave the student without help in getting at Shakspere's chief attributes, his characterization and poetic power. And every practical teacher knows that while every boy can look out hard words from a lexicon for himself, not one in a score can, unhelped, catch points of and realize character, and feel and express the distinctive individuality of each play as a poetic creation.

*From* Prof. EDWARD DOWDEN, LL.D., *of the University of Dublin, Author of "Shakspere: His Mind and Art."*

I incline to think that no edition is likely to be so useful for school and home reading as yours. Your notes contain so much accurate instruction, with so little that is superfluous; you do not neglect the æsthetic study of the play; and in externals, paper, type, binding, etc., you make a book "pleasant to the eyes" (as well as "to be desired to make one wise")—no small matter, I think, with young readers and with old.

*From* EDWIN A. ABBOTT, M.A., *Author of "Shakespearian Grammar."*

I have not seen any edition that compresses so much necessary information into so small a space, nor any that so completely avoids the common faults of commentaries on Shakespeare—needless repetition, superfluous explanation, and unscholar-like ignoring of difficulties.

*From* HIRAM CORSON, M.A., *Professor of Anglo-Saxon and English Literature, Cornell University, Ithaca, N. Y.*

In the way of annotated editions of separate plays of Shakespeare, for educational purposes, I know of none quite up to Rolfe's.

*From* Prof. F. J. CHILD, *of Harvard University.*

I read your "Merchant of Venice" with my class, and found it in every respect an excellent edition. I do not agree with my friend White in the opinion that Shakespeare requires but few notes—that is, if he is to be thoroughly understood. Doubtless he may be enjoyed, and many a hard place slid over. Your notes give all the help a young student requires, and yet the reader for pleasure will easily get at just what he wants. You have indeed been conscientiously concise.

*Under date of July* 25, 1879, Prof. CHILD *adds:* Mr. Rolfe's editions of plays of Shakespeare are very valuable and convenient books, whether for a college class or for private study. I have used them with my students, and I welcome every addition that is made to the series. They show care, research, and good judgment, and are fully up to the time in scholarship. I fully agree with the opinion that experienced teachers have expressed of the excellence of these books.

*From* Rev. A. P. PEABODY, D.D., *Professor in Harvard University.*

I regard your own work as of the highest merit, while you have turned the labors of others to the best possible account. I want to have the higher classes of our schools introduced to Shakespeare chief of all, and then to other standard English authors; but this cannot be done to advantage, unless under a teacher of equally rare gifts and abundant leisure, or through editions specially prepared for such use. I trust that you will have the requisite encouragement to proceed with a work so happily begun.

*From the Examiner and Chronicle, N. Y.*

We repeat what we have often said, that there is no edition of Shakespeare's which seems to us preferable to Mr. Rolfe's. As mere specimens of the printer's and binder's art they are unexcelled, and their other merits are equally high. Mr. Rolfe, having learned by the practical experience of the class-room what aid the average student really needs in order to read Shakespeare intelligently, has put just that amount of aid into his notes, and no more. Having said what needs to be said, he stops there. It is a rare virtue in the editor of a classic, and we are proportionately grateful for it.

*From the N. Y. Times.*

This work has been done so well that it could hardly have been done better. It shows throughout knowledge, taste, discriminating judgment, and, what is rarer and of yet higher value, a sympathetic appreciation of the poet's moods and purposes.

*From the Pacific School Journal, San Francisco.*

This edition of Shakespeare's plays bids fair to be the most valuable aid to the study of English literature yet published. For educational purposes it is beyond praise. Each of the plays is printed in large clear type and on excellent paper. Every difficulty of the text is clearly explained by copious notes. It is remarkable how many new beauties one may discern in Shakespeare with the aid of the glossaries attached to these books. . . . Teachers can do no higher, better work than to inculcate a love for the best literature, and such books as these will best aid them in cultivating a pure and refined taste.

*From the Christian Union, N. Y.*

Mr. W. J. Rolfe's capital edition of Shakespeare—by far the best edition for school and parlor use. We speak after some practical use of it in a village Shakespeare Club. The notes are brief but useful; and the necessary expurgations are managed with discriminating skill.

*From the Academy, London.*

Mr. Rolfe's excellent series of school-editions of the Plays of Shakespeare. . . . Mr. Rolfe's editions differ from some of the English ones in looking on the plays as something more than word-puzzles. They give the student helps and hints on the characters and meanings of the plays, while the word-notes are also full and posted up to the latest date. . . . Mr. Rolfe also adds to each of his books a most useful "Index of Words and Phrases explained."

---

PUBLISHED BY HARPER & BROTHERS, NEW YORK.

☞ *Any of the above works will be sent by mail, postage prepaid, to any part of the United States, on receipt of the price.*

www.ingramcontent.com/pod-product-compliance
Lightning Source LLC
LaVergne TN
LVHW021410110826
845150LV00007B/1861

* 9 7 8 1 4 2 5 5 1 1 2 1 0 *